Miles *Away from* BUTLER

Miles

Away from

BUTLER

How a DNA Test Rewrote My Family's History

STEVEN R. BUTLER

Poor Scholar Publications

POOR SCHOLAR PUBLICATIONS
Richardson, Texas, USA

ISBN 978-0-9981526-6-0

FIRST EDITION

For information about this and other Poor Scholar titles, please visit:

www.watermelon-kid.com/poorscholar/psp.htm

Additional copies of this book are available from:

Amazon.com and other online stores

10 9 8 7 6 5 4 3 2 1

Cover: Looking west from the scenic overlook at Dunlap, Sequatchie County, Tennessee; *author photo.*

This book is dedicated to the memory of my father,
Raymond Joe Butler
(1927-2019)

With thanks to my cousin, Henry Butler, for suggesting the title.

Contents

Introduction

I am a family historian. As I've often told people, I prefer that title to "genealogist" because I have never been satisfied with simply filling in spaces on a pedigree chart with names and dates of birth, death, and marriage, and then moving on to the next generation. To me, the job is much more than that. I have always wanted not only to know my ancestors' names and their vital statistics, but also something about them. *Where* did they live? *Why* did they live there? If they immigrated from another country, *why* did they leave, and *when*—and *how* did they make the journey? *What* did they do for a living? Did they own any property? Fight in a war? Hold an elective office? Well, I think you probably get the idea: I'm just not satisfied with basic facts. *I need details.*

I have also often said that seeking out your ancestors is a lot like Forrest Gump's proverbial box of chocolates, you can't ever be sure of what you're going to get! In 1971, when I began a now-decades-long genealogical journey on the road to uncovering my "roots," I certainly had no idea where it would take me. What would I find out? Was I descended from royalty? From a president? Or, anyone else that was famous in history? Or, something that seemed far more likely—from a long line of mostly ordinary folks?

Although the answer to those questions has turned out to be largely the last one, that doesn't mean that the journey has been uninteresting. Anyone who has spent more than a little time researching their family's history knows very well not only how addictive such activity can be, but also how challenging, how frequently frustrating, and how rewarding too, when you finally find the answers for which you have been looking.

Sometimes though, you just can't find the answers, no matter how hard you try, and occasionally, you find out things you didn't even expect. Several years ago, I was surprised to learn from an Australian friend that long before the British government began sending convicts to penal colonies in the land "Down Under," they "transported" tens of thousands of petty criminals to "His Majesty's Colonies and Dominions in North America"—a verifiable fact which was absent from any of the history textbooks with which I was supplied in either high school or college. I was even more surprised when I unexpectedly discovered some twenty years later that I was descended from one of these immigrants-in-chains—in my case a London chimney sweep who with the help of three friends had committed a burglary, been locked up for a while in the notorious Newgate Prison, and then sentenced to seven years "transportation" to Virginia!

There have been plenty of other surprises along the way. For example, in view of the surnames I initially encountered, I assumed that all my ancestors were British, that is, they were either English, Scottish, Welsh, or Irish. As it happens, most of them were, *but not all.* I also found some Dutch, French, and German ancestors, which really ought not to have been surprising, considering the "melting-pot" that was colonial America. I've likewise discovered that in addition to the ordinary folks—mostly farmers—that I anticipated finding, my family tree is populated by a pirate, at least one colonial governor, a handful of colonial and state legislators, a sheriff, a mayor, a runaway indentured servant, a cowboy, several Revolutionary and Civil War veterans, as well as a member of the United States electoral college!

But of all the unexpected surprises that my years of family history research has revealed, none have come anywhere close to matching the most recent one—the one that prompted me to write this book—and "come close" is definitely the most appropriate way of putting it, because unlike all of my other research surprises, this one hit much closer to home. How? Because unlike all my ancestors who lived and died long before I was born, I had a close personal relationship with two of the three principal parties involved.

But I've said enough for now. *It's time to set the stage!*

Me with my grandmother, Alice Tate Butler, as I remember her in her old age. This photo was taken outside the nursing home where she was living when I visited her during the time I served in the Navy. It's also the place where she died in 1972.

Chapter One

HOW I STARTED OUT ON THE WRONG ROAD

It all began with my grandmother.

In November 1971, shortly after I returned home from nearly four years of service in the United States Navy, I was rummaging through my father and stepmother's attic, looking for some personal mementoes I had left behind, when I unexpectedly came across a box of old photographs belonging to my grandmother, Alice Tate Butler, who was then living in nursing home. Some of the photographs were relatively modern, but many were quite old, dating, I guessed, from the late nineteenth and early twentieth centuries. I remembered seeing some of them when I was a child and spent weekends with my grandmother at her home in old East Dallas, but most of these images were "new" to me.

Soon after, my father brought my grandmother, then eighty-six years old, to stay with us for the weekend. It was the first time I had seen her since my most recent home visit, in January 1970.

After greeting her warmly with a hug and a kiss on her careworn cheek, I told her about the box of photographs I had discovered, confessed that I was curious about them,

1

and asked her if sometime during the next two days she would sit with me and go through the box, so that she could tell me about them. Of course, she agreed.

Ever since that long-ago day, I have regretted that I did not make a tape recording of our conversation, or even take any notes. If I could somehow have known that slightly more than six months later my grandmother would be dead, I'm sure I would have tried to make some record of our conversation, but, like most young people (I was only twenty-two at the time) the thought that someone who had always been a part of my life could suddenly be gone, had never once crossed my mind.

As my grandmother and I sat together on the sofa in my father and stepmother's house, I carefully removed the photos, one-by-one from the box, while she identified the person or persons depicted, and also told me a little about them—whenever she could remember. Family members were no problem, but though the faces of long-ago friends were still familiar, at her advanced age many names were long forgotten. At some point, she also retold me the story, which I had heard before, when I was a child, of how she and her birth family—the Tates—had come to Texas from Alabama when she was a little girl, making the journey, she said, in a mule-drawn covered wagon. Although I have since uncovered evidence that they actually traveled by steamboat and train—my grandmother was not quite three at the time and therefore too young to remember—the story prompted me to wonder aloud how her husband's family— the Butlers—had also come to be in Texas.

Unfortunately, she did not know. The most she could tell me is that her husband, Herman H. Butler, and his two sisters, Lillian and Ozelle, had grown up in Denison, Texas, and that Herman's father's name was William O. Butler, but where they might have lived previously, or where the family had originated, was as much a mystery to her as it was to me.

It was then, at that moment or shortly thereafter, my curiosity aroused, I decided to find out how and when the Butler family came to Texas, and thus a family historian was born.

****

Believe it or not, I actually know the day and date that I began my quest: Monday, December 6, 1971, when I drove to downtown Dallas, where I obtained a certified, photostatic copy of my paternal grandparents' marriage certificate at the Dallas County Records Building on Houston Street. It wasn't until sometime in the early part of 1972, however, after my then-pregnant wife and I had settled into our new apartment in a Dallas suburb, and I had begun my new job as a mail clerk at the Dallas Chamber of Commerce, that I finally found the time, and also the opportunity, to pursue my goal in earnest. Shortly after going to work downtown, I discovered that the main

Dallas Public Library, which was located then at the corner of Harwood Street and Commerce, had a genealogy department on the third floor. Since the library was only a half-mile, ten-minute walk from the office building in which I then worked, at the corner of N. Akard Street and Pacific Avenue, I occasionally spent my lunch hour at the library, doing research instead of eating. Fortunately, part of my duties at the Chamber of Commerce included the making of deliveries in the afternoon, sometimes by car and sometimes on foot, which gave me the opportunity to stop somewhere along the way for a bite to eat on those days that I skipped lunch!

Unfortunately, because I had practically no clues to go on, all I managed to find out at first, from examining old Dallas city directories, was that Herman Butler and his father, William O. Butler, had come to live in Dallas around 1900, possibly a year earlier, and that they had initially resided in the heart of what had become by mid-century a thriving business district dominated by tall skyscrapers.

My grandmother had already told me that after leaving Alabama, her family—the Tates—had lived for a while in the small West Texas town of Vernon. City directories verified that they left Vernon and came to in Dallas in 1890. Directory listings also confirmed that both Herman Butler and his father, William, were carpenters by trade, whereas among other things, my other paternal great-grandfather, Isaac H. Tate, had once operated a vegetable stand on Elm Street, in the heart of downtown Dallas.

The Tate family Bible, which contained the birth, death and marriage dates of my grandmother's parents, as well as all her brothers and sisters, was also in a box at my father and stepmother's house, and it too was useful, but of course, it told me nothing at all about the Butler family, the origins of which would remain a seemingly unsolvable mystery for the next five years.

On Sunday, May 28, 1972, my grandmother died at the nursing home where she had resided during the last few years of her life. Her passing filled me with a tremendous sense of personal loss, not only because she was one of the few people in the world at that time who I deeply loved, but also because it ended any further chance that she could help me in my search for our family's "roots." Unfortunately, although I didn't know it at the time, she also took a long-hidden secret to her grave—which if revealed before her death, would have spared me the enormous amount of time, money, and effort that I expended over the next nearly forty-seven years, to paraphrase a popular song of the era, "looking for ancestors in all the wrong places."

****

Between the fall of 1972—when I enrolled as a student at the then-new Richland College in Northeast Dallas—and the late summer of 1976—when I was graduated with a bachelor's degree in History from Rhode Island College in Providence, Rhode Island—I had neither the time nor the opportunity to do any further family history research. In September 1976, however, as soon as my wife and toddler son and I returned to Dallas, I started the search anew.

Unfortunately, insofar as the Butler side of my family was concerned, after four years I still had practically nothing to go on. Then one day, it suddenly occurred to me that I was just as much my mother's son as my father's, and that there was no good reason why I shouldn't also look into the history of *her* side of the family. Soon after, I temporarily abandoned the search for my paternal "roots" to research my maternal lineage instead. It turned out to be a good decision, not least because it taught me that if you ever hope to make any progress as a family historian, you must be like water, that is, you should take the path of least resistance. Enthusiastically and ably assisted by an aunt, Inez Jenkins Hickman, whose help I sought after my mother showed absolutely no interest in the project, I made great strides within only a few short months.

Although the hunt for my maternal ancestors turned out to be much more rewarding that I had anticipated, I did not forget about my paternal ancestry altogether. In the late summer of 1977, I renewed my efforts by writing a letter to Anne Hunt, who was then the genealogical columnist for the *Dallas Morning News*, asking her to publish a query in which I sought to find someone who might be able to help me learn more about the family whose surname I bear. I realized it was a long shot, but I figured I had nothing to lose by trying, and who knew? Maybe something would come of it.

Up to that time, what little I knew about the Butler family came from a relative (no pun intended) handful of sources: Bits of information that my grandmother had passed on to me before she died in 1972; my grandfather Herman's death certificate; his grave marker at Forest Lawn cemetery in Dallas; some census records; and some Dallas city directory entries. All I really knew at that time, or thought I knew, was that my great-grandfather, William O. Butler, was born about 1856—but I didn't know where— and that his son, Herman H. Butler, was born in 1878, purportedly in Mexia, Texas, and that the Butlers had lived in Denison before the family reached Dallas sometime around the turn of the twentieth century.

Although I hoped that my letter to the *Dallas Morning News* would have results, deep down I didn't really expect any. Consequently, I was astonished when on the very same day my query was published (Thursday, September 15, 1977), I received a phone call from an elderly woman named Tressa Butler, who told me that we were related, but not through the Butler side of the family, because, as she explained, Butler was her married, not maiden, name.

Initially, I was reluctant to get my hopes up, but then as she continued talking, telling me things about my family that only someone related to me could possibly know—information that wasn't mentioned in the genealogy column query—I realized that Mrs. Butler was genuine!

Not surprisingly, I went to see her as soon as I could, which was Saturday, September 30, 1977, a little more than two weeks following the publication of my letter in the paper.

When I arrived at Mrs. Butler's home in the "M" streets section of Dallas, her then-middle-aged daughter greeted me at the door and invited me in. After meeting Tressa and exchanging pleasantries, the discoveries began.

One of the first things Tressa told me is that she and I were related through her grandmother—a woman named Lucy Ann Babb—who was also Herman Butler's grandmother. This made Tressa and I second cousins, twice removed.

I also learned from Tressa that in 1925 her father, Arthur Babb—my first cousin, three times removed (or so I then thought)—had written a book that told the story of his life. Begun about two weeks before his sixtieth birthday, Arthur wrote in its preface:

"It has often occurred to me that there are a number of things that transpire during our lives of more or less interest to ourselves & others that we should make note of; a kind of setting 'milestones,' so to speak."

"Cellini said that 'Every man that had proved himself superior to those of his time should write an autobiography.'"

"This qualification would relieve many of us of the task. However, I do think that it would at least be interesting for each of us to make some record of himself & of things that have transpired in his time that would be of interest in the future. It is with this in mind that I make the succeeding notes."

When Tressa showed me Arthur's book, hand-written in pencil, I was pleased to see that he had not only told his own life story, but also listed the births, deaths, and marriages of several relatives, including Herman Butler, his sisters and their parents, William and Alice Butler, the very same people I had mentioned in my newspaper query!

Arthur's book also provided valuable clues for further research. For example, although it was true that the Butler family had once lived near Mexia, in Limestone County, thanks to Arthur, I learned that they had first resided in neighboring Freestone County, where the town of Fairfield, which I had never heard of before 1977, is the county seat. The next time I visited the downtown Dallas public library, I examined the 1860 federal census for Freestone County, where I found Herman Butler's father, William, listed as a four-year-old child in a household headed by a thirty-six-year-old carpenter named Alfred Butler, apparently my great-great-grandfather, with a wife named Mary, and four other children. Alfred was missing from the 1870 federal census, which suggested that he died in the Civil War, but Mary and all her children, including William, by then fourteen, were there.

Long story short: Thanks to Arthur Babb, a man I never met—although our lifetimes slightly overlapped (I was born two years before he died)—I was eventually able to add another generation of Butlers to my family tree, as well as a host of associated paternal ancestors, whose surnames were Owen and Stanley. At last, I had found the breakthrough for which I had been looking!

Arthur's book also enabled me to correct some errors. According to both his death certificate and his headstone in Forest Lawn Cemetery, Herman Butler was born in 1878. That's because my grandmother, who obviously wasn't present when her husband was born, was the person who reported his death, but in doing so she made a mistake. Herman's actual birth year was 1880, which I first saw written in Arthur's book, and afterward confirmed through federal census and other public records.

In his "Life Book," Arthur Babb also revealed that his maternal grandfather, Madison Owen, had served with General Winfield Scott's army during the War with Mexico in 1847. Tressa told me further that Owen had kept a diary, which she previously had in her possession, but had loaned it several years earlier to a distant relative. Unfortunately, she couldn't remember who. Consequently,

I never saw it, but thankfully, Arthur had transcribed a few lines and included them in his book.

It was also around this same time—the fall of 1977—that I reached out, by mail, to Fred Garrett, one of the sons of Herman Butler's sister, Lillian Butler Garrett, and also to Ralph Storey, one of the sons of Herman's other sister, Ozelle Butler Storey. Although neither Fred nor Ralph were particularly interested in family history, Ralph put me in touch with his sixty-nine-year-old sister, Marian Storey Wood, who was not only very interested in my research, but also invited me to visit her and her husband, Albert, in East Texas, where they owned some rural property. I never went, however, because at the time I did not own a reliable automobile and feared breaking down in the middle of nowhere. Marian and I would eventually meet, but it would have to wait a while.

Unfortunately, no sooner had I made these contacts, than I had to set aside my research again, this time for five years. From December 1977 through December 1982, my family and I lived in London, England, where I worked for the American Express Company. During that entire period, I was unable, in that pre-Internet era, to do any further research, since all the records I needed to access were in the United States.

Less than two months after our return, however, I resumed my quest. In February 1983, with the youngest of my two sons in tow, I visited Fairfield, Texas, for the first time.

There, in the Freestone County courthouse, I located some deed records for Alfred Butler, as well as the marriage certificate of his son, William O. Butler and William's wife, Virginia Alice Owen—who I afterward learned was William's first cousin. I also found a deed for Alfred Butler's mother-in-law, Elizabeth Stanley. Later, using Sanborn fire insurance maps and a vintage Freestone County property map, I was able to pinpoint the precise locations of her property, as well as Alfred Butler's.

During a subsequent visit to Fairfield, I visited the Freestone County Museum, where the curator gave me a photocopy of a page from an old general store account book, detailing the Alfred Butler family's purchases for the year 1859. For me, the early-to-mid 1980s were a heady time, because little-by-little, the story of the Butler family in Texas was being revealed.

In 1986, during a visit to the eighth floor Genealogy Department of the new downtown Dallas Public Library on Jackson Street, I sought to confirm Madison Owen's service in the U.S.-Mexican War. When I was unable to find his name in any of the microfilmed service records (I later learned that he was not a soldier, but rather a civilian teamster, driving wagons for the army), I decided to see if any of my other ancestors had served in that war.

To my surprise, I discovered that Alfred Butler, who I had earlier found in census records thanks to clues provided by Arthur Babb's book, *was* listed in both the U.S.-Mexican

12

war service and bounty land records. Furthermore, his widow, Mary F. Butler, had applied for a federal pension in the 1880s. After I sent for and received copies of these records from the National Archives in Washington, D.C., I learned that Alfred Butler had been born about 1824 in Bertie County, North Carolina, that he had enlisted in Greene County, Alabama, that he had first arrived in Texas, as a soldier, in 1846, and that he had lived briefly in Union County, Arkansas, before returning to Texas in 1852, this time to make a home.

Discovering that Alfred Butler was a soldier in the Mexican War was for me like tossing a rock into a pond. What followed was the so-called "ripple effect."

In 1989, after learning that there were no lineage societies in the United States with membership based on Mexican War veteran ancestry—apart from the Aztec Club, which was limited to the descendants of officers only—I decided to do something ambitious, something which in hindsight I doubt very much I would have done if I could have known then how much of my time and effort it was going to take and how much controversy was potentially involved; and there is no question that I would not have done it if I had known then the secret that my grandmother took to her grave: I initiated the founding of The Descendants of Mexican War Veterans (DMWV), a national lineage society that I went on to serve as President for twelve long years—from 1989 to 2001—a society which is now (as of 2019) thirty years old.

During the dozen years I served as President of the DMWV, in addition to almost single-handedly planning and implementing the society's activities, I did an enormous amount of research about the U.S.-Mexican War, which I initially knew very little about, so that I could knowledgeably write articles for the DMWV's bi-annual publication, *Mexican War Journal*, of which I was the editor. Doing so led me to discover the Special Collections library at the University of Texas at Arlington, which houses an abundance of documentary material relating to the war. There, I met archivists and historians who encouraged me to enroll in graduate school, which I finally did in 1997, earning a master's degree from UTA in 1999 and a doctorate in 2006.

Throughout this same period, I also made several trips to the Lower Rio Grande Valley, primarily to attend history conferences in Brownsville, Texas and Matamoros, Mexico, which in turn led me to become an unpaid advisor to KERA-TV's U.S.-Mexican War documentary team. When the documentary finally aired on PBS in 1998, I was quite proud to see my name in the credits, and also in the introduction of the companion book.

Simultaneously, a Brownsville businessman, Walter Plitt, spearheaded an effort to have the Palo Alto Battlefield turned into a national historic park, a goal that was eventually achieved. Under my leadership, the DMWV gave its wholehearted support to this endeavor, and Walter and I soon became friends. Inspired by his example and at my suggestion, the DMWV turned its attention to other U.S.-Mexican War sites in the Lower Rio Grande Valley. In 1996, the organization paid for the erecting of a flagpole at the site of Zachary Taylor's Fort Texas, later called Fort Brown, which was located on the north bank of the Rio Grande, opposite the city of Matamoros in Mexico. One of my proudest moments was the day in May 1996, when the flagpole dedication ceremony was held and I was one of the keynote speakers, along with the Mayor of Brownsville and Congressman Solomon Ortiz.

During my visits to South Texas, I also conducted personal research. On one occasion, accompanied by my father, and another, accompanied by my youngest son, I explored the desolate spot near the mouth of the Rio Grande, where Alfred Butler and his fellow Alabama Volunteers had encamped in the summer of 1846. Another proud moment was the day in 1997 when I participated in the dedication of a Texas State Historical Commission marker at the site of what was known in 1846 as "Camp Belknap"—a marker the placement of which I had initiated, and which was paid for by the DMWV. I also visited nearby Brazos Santiago, the spot where the First Alabama regiment had come ashore on Independence Day, 1846—the day that Private Alfred Butler first arrived in Texas.

In the late spring of 1996 and again in 1997, accompanied by my recently-retired father, I traveled to Eutaw, the seat of Greene County, Alabama, where I not only did some research in the county courthouse, but also, on the second trip, had the honor of addressing a meeting of the Greene County Historical Society, where my topic was the "Eutaw Rangers"—a company of soldiers from that town who had volunteered for service in the U.S.-Mexican War, a group that included Alfred Butler. Research in the Alabama State Archives in Montgomery resulted in my authoring a book, *Alabama Volunteers in the Mexican War*, which was published by the DMWV. It included a complete roster of every soldier from Alabama who had served in that conflict, transcribed from National Archives microfilm that I paid for myself, and then afterward donated to the DMWV. I also edited the diaries and letters of two Alabama solders—the captain who had led the "Eutaw Rangers," Sydenham Moore, and a private soldier, Stephen Nunnelee—for publication by the DMWV.

In 1998, to personally honor Alfred Butler, I ordered a government headstone from the Veterans Administration, and although the precise location of his unmarked grave is unknown, I arranged for it to be placed in the Fairfield City Cemetery, where it is likely he was buried when he died from some unknown illness in 1860. More than a decade later, in 2010, I had a headstone made for Alfred's son. William O. Butler—paid for by me, my father, and my cousin Henry Butler—which was placed at the head of his grave in Dallas' Oakland Cemetery.

These efforts to honor my ancestors even reached into my personal life. For nearly two decades my email address was "texian1846," a name that was deliberately chosen to pay homage to the fact that Alfred Butler, as a soldier in the U.S-Mexican War, had first arrived in Texas in 1846, its first full year of statehood.

There are several other things I did, or in some cases nearly did, as a consequence of immersing myself in my family's history, too numerous to recount in their entirety, but here a few examples: In the mid-1980s, for instance, I took out a bank loan to buy ten acres of land in Freestone County, Texas, where Alfred Butler and his family had settled in the early 1850s—but the deal fell through when the seller had to pull out, owing to divorce proceedings. Around this same time, I also seriously considered relocating my family to either Sherman or Denison, Texas, because my Butler and Stanley ancestors had also once lived in Grayson County.

Grayson County was also one of the places where in the 1990s, assisted by my oldest son, I made a videotaped family history documentary based on a Butler family history book that I wrote and self-published in 1994, entitled *A Home in Texas*, Parts of the documentary were videotaped in Dallas and Fairfield as well.

Although my wife and I eventually bought a home in a Dallas suburb instead, I continued to visit Grayson County from time-to-time, either to do research at the Denison and Sherman public libraries, or to search for the precise location of the farm that had been bought in 1885 by Arthur Babb's mother, Lucy Ann—my supposed great-

great-grandmother. In the spring of 2014, using a vintage county map, I finally found it. After I contacted the present owner, she very graciously invited me to visit, which I did with my oldest son and grandson. I made a second visit to what Arthur Babb had called the "Pike's Peak Farm" (on account of its hilltop setting), with my elderly father, in December 2015.

To summarize: For nearly half a century I not only thoroughly invested myself, my time, my effort, and my money into learning all that I could about my Butler ancestors, but also incorporated that knowledge into my personal life—*and then one day in 2019, I made the most unexpected discovery of my life, one that would end up rewriting a quarter of my family's history as I then knew it.*

Chapter Two
HOW I DISCOVERED THE FAMILY SECRET

In 2014, I decided to order an Ancestry.com DNA kit. I did so for two reasons. First, I wanted to confirm what I already believed to be true: That my ancestors were largely British, French, German, and Dutch. Secondly, I hoped that the list of DNA matches that Ancestry promised to provide would allow me to contact other researchers to who I was related, in order to share information, and perhaps advance our knowledge of the ancestors we had in common.

The process is remarkably easy. The company analyzes your DNA, after extracting it from a small sample of saliva or "spit," and then posts the results in your account on their website. Unfortunately, because I did not provide enough saliva initially, Ancestry had to send me a new kit, so that I could start over. Consequently, it was not until June 2015 that I finally received the results for which I had been anxiously waiting.

Insofar as my ethnicity was concerned, there were no major surprises, only confirmation of what my documentary research had already told me, namely that my genetic ethnicity was largely British, with a little bit of French, Dutch, and German ancestry thrown into the mix.

My initial results also indicated that I possessed a large percentage of Scandinavian ancestry, which seemed strange to me as there were no Scandinavian surnames in my family tree. I reasoned that it must go back to the time when the Vikings first raided and then settled in England. Sometime later, Ancestry.com reassessed my results and the Scandinavian ancestry completely disappeared. I had thought it might be a mistake. (It has since reappeared in a newer assessment, but in a much smaller percentage than previously posted.)

The company also provides you with a list of people with whom you share DNA. Some of my matches were cousins whose names I immediately recognized, people with whom I had already communicated regarding our mutual heritage, but most of the others had surnames that weren't familiar at all. One small group of matches that stood out from all the others were the four people whose last name was Miles. One of these was identified as a 2nd to 3rd cousin. The other three were identified as 3rd to 4th cousins.

At first, I didn't think anything of it, assuming that they were probably members of a family with whom I shared a common ancestor somewhere in the distant past. You might think that I would have contacted them to ask, but since they all had a family tree posted online, I contented myself with examining those instead. When I couldn't see any connection, and also because none of the four had researched their lines as extensively as I had, I just didn't

20

think it would be worthwhile to communicate with any of them at that particular time. I reasoned that probably, sooner or later, I would find the connection, and when and/or if I did, I would contact them then.

In the meantime, I paid for my wife, my youngest son, and my father to take the Ancestry.com DNA test. No surprises emerged, either large or small, but my wife, who is a natural blonde and has blue eyes, was disappointed when the test revealed no Scandinavian ancestry, as she had expected.

In 2017, someone I know who had also taken an Ancestry DNA test told me that certain living relatives this person expected to see in the provided list of matches weren't there, and also that their ethnicity estimate included lots of DNA from an unexpected place. The only way to explain it was that this person's biological father was someone other than the man that raised them, which I said as tactfully as possible. Surprising, yes, but there was no choice other than to accept it. Later, this person speculated that their actual father was most likely a man who had known their mother while undergoing military training in the state where their mother lived during World War II, and in early 2019, using the clues my acquaintance provided, I was not only able to identify the man by name, but also to provide some details about his life. Unfortunately, he was deceased, but this information was welcomed, and I was thanked for my help. *Thank goodness, I thought at the time, nothing like that had happened to me!*

Then, in late 2018, I decided to send for a 23 and Me DNA kit. I did so for two reasons. First, because a maternal-line cousin encouraged me. A few months earlier, when she had her own DNA analyzed by 23 and Me, she discovered that she was related to two women whose names were completely unfamiliar to her. When she found out further that they were twins, born in Chicago in the early 1960s, who had been given up for adoption by their birth mother, my cousin began to wonder if *my* mother, who was a single parent living in Chicago at that time, might be *their* mother. In other words, she thought they might be my long-lost half-sisters.

Although I thought it was highly unlikely that my mother had become pregnant out of wedlock (she was then divorced from my first stepfather), given up her twin daughters for adoption, and then had somehow managed to hide the fact from her entire family, including me, I agreed to take the test.

I also took the 23 and Me test because I thought it might help me find my elusive Butler ancestors. At the time, I had reason to believe that the Butlers had intermarried with a Johnson family that lived in Alabama in the early nineteenth century, but was unable to find any documentation to verify it. If I could find some way to prove this supposition, it would take my Butler line back at least two more generations. Earlier, I had communicated with a Johnson family researcher on Ancestry.com about the possible connection between the two families. When she told me that she had a sibling who had taken the 23 and Me DNA test, I hoped my own results would prove the connection.

When I finally received my 23 and Me results in February 2019, I was very disappointed to learn that I wasn't a match to the Johnson family after all. At the same time, I was relieved when the twins my cousin had worried about did *not* turn out to be my sisters!

Three of my closest 23 and Me matches were people whose names I immediately recognized. One was the maternal-line first cousin who had encouraged me to send for the kit, her son, and Aletha Hicks, a paternal-line first cousin once-removed, who is my Aunt Margaret's granddaughter. Aletha and I already knew one another, and had corresponded on a few occasions in the past.

My close matches also included a woman whose name was completely unfamiliar—Beverly Lumpkin—identified in the list as a first or second cousin. I reasoned that Lumpkin was probably her married name (which as it turned out, it *was*), which might account for it being unknown to me.

Although I contacted Aletha through the 23 and Me website messaging system, to say "hi" and ask if she remembered me (she did), I did not immediately contact Beverly, largely because I wasn't sure how she fit into the picture, and thought it could wait till later.

The very same day that my 23 and Me DNA test results became available, I shared the news with another paternal-line cousin, Richard Garrett, with whom I had been communicating on-and-off for several years (although we've never actually met in person). A little less than a month later, after learning from Richard that he had taken both the 23 and Me and the Ancestry.com DNA tests, I looked for him in my matches on both websites, but for some odd reason he wasn't there. Here is what I wrote to him, by email, that very same day:

> *Rich:*
> *I am not finding you among my matches on either 23 and Me or Ancestry.*
>
> *You should be there as a second cousin because we share a set of great-grandparents (William O. Butler and Virginia Alice Owen).*
>
> *This worries me because if we are not a DNA match, and should be, then what could be the explanation?*
>
> *Best,*
> *Steve*

In his reply to me, Richard could offer no explanation for this anomaly either, but then later, as I began to remember some things that he had told me earlier about his parents, I began to think I had figured out the answer. On March 30, I sent him another email:

I hope you won't mind me saying this, but since we have both had both the Ancestry and 23 and Me DNA tests, and neither of us is a match to the other with either test, I think the only conclusion we can reach is that we are not actually cousins.

I recall you telling me that after your parents were divorced, your mother moved, with you, back to Ohio and that you grew up among her relatives, and not the Garretts.

Did your mother ever tell you why her marriage to Charles Garrett failed? I think the fact that we are not showing up as DNA matches may go a long way toward explaining what happened, even if we have no details. Charles Garrett's mother was most certainly Lillian Butler. Therefore, if you had Butler ancestry, you should show up as a match to me, since my grandfather, Herman Butler, was Lillian's brother.

After telling Richard, as gently and as carefully as I could, that I believed the only possible answer was that his biological father was someone other than the man he had always thought, and that I knew someone else to who this same sort of thing had happened, I concluded my email with these words:

I'm sure this must have crossed your mind. I can think of no other plausible explanation.

In response, Richard wrote: "Thank you for the reply! And yes, your conclusion is the correct one I am sure." But then Richard sent me, by email, a screenshot of his 23 and Me DNA matches.

The very first thing I noticed is that my cousin, Aletha, was right at the top of Richard's 23 and Me DNA matches! That's odd, I thought. How could it be, I wondered, that Aletha is a match to both me and Richard, but Richard and I are not a match to each other? It just didn't make sense.

After some careful thought on the matter, I began to realize that there was only one possible explanation. Initially, I had deduced that Richard was the one without any Butler ancestry, that his father was not the man he thought he was, but what if I was wrong about that? What if *I* was the one without Butler ancestry?

My grandmother, Alice Tate Butler, was Aletha's great-grandmother, but my grandmother was not related in any way to Richard since Butler was her married name, not her maiden name. However, my grandmother's husband, Herman H. Butler, was not only the brother of Richard's grandmother, Lillian Butler Garrett, but also Aletha's great-grandfather.

Here's what I wrote to Richard, in an email, on March 30, 2019:

It occurred to me: What if I am the one who doesn't have any Butler DNA?

My grandfather was Herman H. Butler (or so I've always thought). Your grandmother was Herman's sister, Lillian Butler Garrett. Their father was William O. Butler.

Aletha Hicks' grandmother was Herman Butler's daughter, my father's sister, Margaret Butler Vance.

But what if Herman Butler was not my father's father? What if my grandmother is the one who had [an extramarital relationship]?

In other words, what if my dad and his sister, Margaret had the same mother, but not the same father. In that case, I could be related to Aletha through my grandmother, Alice Tate Butler, and you could be related to Aletha through Herman and Lillian Butler's side of the family. That would mean that I'm the one, not you, with no Butler DNA.

This is just the opposite of what we, or I, thought earlier.

I plotted it out on paper. It's the only explanation that makes sense, that I can think of.

Does this scenario make sense? Am I overlooking something?

That very same day, I had also sent a message, through the 23 and Me website, to Beverly Lumpkin, saying that I was trying to figure out how we were related, and asking if the surnames Butler or Tate were familiar to her. She wrote back to say that an aunt on her dad's side of her family had married a Butler, but I couldn't see how that would make us related. Then, I noticed that the surname Miles was one of a few that Beverly had listed in her 23 and Me profile as surnames she was researching.

Remembering that there were four people with the surname Miles in my list of Ancestry.com DNA matches, and also because my father was born in 1927, on a hunch I decided to examine a copy of the 1927 Dallas City Directory on Ancestry.com, to see if there was anyone with the surname Miles living in the East Dallas neighborhood where my father was born and raised. As it turned out there *was*, and in point of fact, the information I uncovered was even more incredible than I had bargained for! Sure enough, living right next door to Herman and Alice Butler, who resided at 1432 Rowan Avenue, was the family of a man named C. W. Miles. A little more research revealed that the initials "C. W." stood for Charles Wesley, and that he was a native of Tennessee, born in 1885.

On Sunday, March 31—by coincidence the very same day that my father moved into a North Dallas retirement home—I sent Beverly Lumpkin another message through the 23 and Me website, saying that I had seen the surname Miles in her family tree and asking if Charles Wesley Miles, born in Tennessee, was anywhere in it. She soon replied, "He was my grandfather on my mom's side."

At that moment, I knew that I had solved the mystery of why Aletha was related to both Richard and me without he and I being related to each other, that the explanation I had proposed to Richard in my email was the correct one: *In short, my grandfather was not Herman Butler. My actual grandfather—my father's biological father—was clearly Charles Wesley Miles!*

To say that I was stunned by this news would be putting it mildly. Not once in my entire life up to that point had I ever heard even the least hint or whisper that my grandmother had had an extramarital relationship of some kind with her next-door neighbor in 1927. But there it was, the truth uncovered after more than ninety-one years of secrecy and staring me in the face, so to speak. There was no denying it. Beverly wasn't the only one with the surname Miles in her family tree to who I was a DNA match. *It had to be true.* There was no other plausible explanation.

Later that same day, I sent another message to Beverly, asking her mother's name and also asking her to contact me through my email address, saying that I had some information about her grandfather and that she would almost certainly find it "incredible."

Just past 9 p.m. that night, Beverly sent me an email, saying "Tell me more!" And so, I did:

> *Beverly:*
> *I hope you are sitting down, because I am about to drop a genealogical bombshell on you, and I assure you, this is no April Fool's Day joke, although I have to say that right now, I'm feeling a bit like a fool.*
>
> *Like me, you have probably been wondering how you and I could possibly be related, yet there we are, on each other's 23 and Me list of DNA matches.*

Well, without going into too many details, which I can do later, the truth of the matter is that you and I are not second cousins, as it says on 23 and Me. We are in fact first cousins, because we share the same grandfather, Charles Wesley Miles.

For all my life, until today (and I am nearly 70 years old), I believed that a man named Herman H. Butler was my grandfather. In 1927, he lived with my grandmother, Alice Tate Butler, at 1432 Rowan Avenue in East Dallas. This is the place where my father, Raymond Joe Butler, now 91 years old, was born.

In 1927, Charles W. Miles and his wife Lillian, and their children, lived at 1426 Rowan Avenue, right next door to Herman and Alice Butler and their family.

I am now 100 percent certain that my grandmother Alice...had an [extramarital relationship of some kind] with Charles W. Miles, and the result was my father, born on December 21, 1927.

I would not be telling you this if I was not absolutely certain. I did a lot of research, and also compared the results of DNA tests with people who I had believed were my cousins, only to find that they weren't. But you are.

I cannot begin to tell you how many years of research I have devoted to tracking down my Butler ancestors, only to find [this out] at this late date.

It's overwhelming to say the least and I dare not tell my father, who just moved into an old folks' home in North Dallas this very day! It would almost certainly devastate him.

I keep thinking it is all just a dream and that any minute I will wake up and all the ancestors on my father's side that I thought I had will be there again, but I know that's not going to happen. This is no dream.

As I had told Richard, I mentioned to Beverly that I knew someone to which this sort of thing had happened and added that I had felt sorry for that person.

Now I am feeling bad for myself, but at the same time strangely excited and even, for a number of reasons, a little liberated.

This was completely unexpected.

So now you know.

Oh, one more thing. I live in Richardson, Texas. If my research is correct, you also reside in the Dallas area. If that's the case, I would like very much, once all this has sunk in, to meet with you sometime in the near future. I would especially like to know if you have any photos of our grandfather and if you have any scanned, could you send them in an email?

Thank you.

Steven Butler

The next morning, Beverly replied to my email. I hadn't been sure how she would take it, but thankfully, her response was very positive. "This is exciting, especially for you! Will send some pics to you. When would you like to meet and where? I live in Mesquite. Anywhere in Dallas would be good."

After I gave Beverly my mobile phone number, we arranged, by text messaging, to meet at the TGI Fridays in Mesquite, Texas, near Town East Mall, at 11:30 a.m. on Friday, April 19, for lunch.

In the meantime, Beverly and I exchanged a lot of both personal and family information by email, and I also did a tremendous amount of online family history research, which enabled me to become much better acquainted with my "new" family as well as my "new" ancestors. Of course, they weren't actually "new" at all, they were there all along. I just didn't know about them. Beverly also sent me some digitized photographs of our grandfather and other family members I had never seen before, which were helpful to my research.

Soon after I made this startling discovery, I shared the news, by email, with Richard Garrett, and expressed regret that he and I weren't cousins after all. Richard was very kind, saying that he would always consider me his "honorary" cousin.

I also shared the news, by email, with my cousin Henry Butler, who lives out-of-state, and who in light of my discovery, I now know is my half-cousin, since we share only one grandparent, not two. Thankfully, Henry also took it well, and was very kind and supportive.

Because I had decided to withhold this information from my father, I told no one in my family who had any regular direct contact with him. My fear was that someone might make some sort of off-hand remark in his presence and unintentionally "let the cat out of the bag." I tried to imagine how I would feel at the age of ninety-one if I suddenly discovered not only that my father was not who I had always thought, but also that my mother had deliberately concealed this fact from me. I'm sure I wouldn't want to believe it. At first, even I wished it wasn't true, but there could be no doubt about it. *There was no other way to explain why Beverly Lumpkin was my cousin and Richard Garrett wasn't.*

Before I go any further with this story, I need to explain why I told my "new" cousin Beverly that "for a number of reasons," I felt "a little liberated" by the news.

Herman H. Butler, the man I'd thought for nearly seventy years was my grandfather, was someone I'm not sure I would have liked very much, if I had known him, which of course I didn't because he died fourteen years before I was born. Why? Because it was no secret in our family that during the 1920s, Herman had been an active member of the Ku Klux Klan in Dallas and was clearly, according to other stories I heard about him, a sexist as well as a racist. This certainly didn't make him exceptional, since most working-class white Southern males of his era were equally intolerant, but I had long considered these things, especially his membership in the KKK, both embarrassing and shameful. The knowledge that I was not actually his grandson was what made the news so "liberating" to me.

Four days after I discovered the family secret, I wrote a letter to one of the few people I had entrusted with the secret, someone who had no regular direct contact with my father. In the letter, I confided my feelings about the matter, in the hope that it would help me come to terms with the emotional challenge that this most recent genealogical discovery presented. Here, in part (and with some slight modifications) is what I said:

> I'm writing this letter [in the hope that it will help] me...come to terms with the latest revelation about our family's history...[I am especially]...relieved to learn that...a man who belonged to the Ku Klux Klan [is not my actual grandfather]...All my life, even though his activities had nothing to do with me personally, I kept that secret from anyone outside the family, because of the shame that I felt about it. It is liberating to know that I no longer need to do so.

> At the same time, this latest revelation initially left me feeling unsettled. For the past few days, I've been feeling as if someone close to me had died.

34

After much reflection...I am at last beginning to come to terms with it. It seems to me now that the problem is not so much what I learned recently, but rather the timing of the discovery that has made it hard to take.

Ironically, it was a conversation that I had with my grandmother in November 1971, not long after I got out of the Navy, that led me to seek out the Butler family origins. After hearing her tell how her family— the Tates—had come to Texas from Alabama when she was a little girl, I asked her if she knew where the Butlers had come from. She said that all she knew was that her husband, Herman Butler, had grown up in Denison, and she didn't even know much about that. That's when I decided to try to find out, and eventually I did. I wish now, however, that before I got too far along that path, that she...had taken me aside and told me what I now know to be true, that my grandfather wasn't Herman Butler, but rather a man named Charlie Miles. If I had known that from the start, I probably would have simply accepted it as the fact that it is, and I certainly would not have expended so much effort over the past nearly five decades trying to learn more about the Butler family's origins. But no one told me. Why? Well, my father didn't because he simply didn't know. And my grandmother did not tell him, or me, because—well, I don't know why.

But I can guess. One possible explanation is that she might have honestly believed, in spite of her indiscretion, that Herman Butler was [my father's] father. Another possibility is that although she was uncertain who his father was, she thought it best, as they say, "to let sleeping dogs lie." For either her, or Charlie (if he knew), to acknowledge even the possibility that he, and not Herman, was [my father's] father, could have, and almost certainly would have, led to the dissolution of not just one, but two marriages. Additionally, my grandmother, and my father too, would almost certainly have suffered the ill effects of the social stigma that would have accompanied such a revelation. Unfortunately, there is no way for us now to know who knew what, or whether my grandmother alone, or she and Charlie together, decided to keep silent about it.

All [that anyone] can know with certainty is that when [my father] was born, on his birth certificate Herman Butler was named as his father and [he] ended up with Butler as his surname, rather that the surname of the man we now know to be his biological father. Although Herman may or may not have done so knowingly, in effect he adopted [my father] and insofar as I know, he always treated him as his own child. I have no way of knowing for sure, but I'd be willing to bet that Herman simply didn't know, or if he suspected, he kept his suspicions to himself.

Obviously, [my father] did not know that Herman was not his actual dad and so, when I was born, he happily passed on the Butler surname to me [and my two half-brothers], just as I passed it on to [my two sons. and my oldest son to my grandsons]. The result is that legally...we have been Butlers for four generations, and that's an awfully long time.

Upon reflection, I realize now that in effect, this puts [all who are affected] in pretty much the same category as an orphan who was legally adopted and given the surname of their adoptive parents. I would be willing to bet that even after someone learns in either childhood or early adulthood that they are adopted, in most cases they not only keep their adoptive family's surname, but knowingly and deliberately pass it on to their own children. Personally, I am quite happy with the surname Butler. It has identified me for nearly seventy years and I intend for it to do so until the end of my life. The fact that if my biological grandparents had been married to each other instead of to other partners, my surname would be different, is of no consequence now, because that's not what happened, and [the past can't be changed].

The only thing [that has] changed is that unlike [my father]...future generations of Butlers will know how [they] got [that] name...The important thing is that... the change [is known], and the circumstances that prompted it. I think...the negative feelings that [initially overwhelmed me] were fueled by the fact that the circumstances which led [to the change] had been previously unknown.

[I'm also mindful of the fact that] if things had not happened the way they did, then [neither me, nor my father, nor my sons, nor my grandsons]—would be alive today. I am grateful for my life, and [for all of theirs as well].

I feel a whole lot better[now], and I'm not going to let this most recent discovery bother me anymore.

In closing, I'll just add that you [may be interested] to know that the DNA tests I have taken have shown no other surprises. In short, there is no doubt whatever that [everyone] on my father's side [of the family]...are descended from the Tates and all their associated families, as well as from all the families I have researched on my mother's side.

Next week, I plan to meet in person with one of [my] "new" cousins, a granddaughter of Charlie Miles, who is about my age. We have been in contact with one another by email. Should be interesting. I'll let you know how that goes.

After writing this letter, I began too to think of all the many people in the world who had either deliberately changed their surnames, or had had them changed for them, and were quite happy with the change. One example are the two U.S. presidents—Gerald R. Ford and Bill Clinton—who deliberately adopted their stepfather's surname. In fact, Gerald Ford, whose birth name was Leslie Lynch King, Jr., not only adopted his stepfather's surname, but also his first and middle name, becoming Gerald Rudolph Ford, Jr.

Similarly, President Bill Clinton got his start in life as William Jefferson Blythe, III. After his father died in an automobile accident and his widowed mother married an Arkansas businessman named Roger Clinton, little Billy

Blythe chose to be known from thereon as Bill Clinton, the surname he formally adopted at age fifteen, and then later passed on to his daughter, Chelsea Clinton.

By the same token, the actor John Wayne was born Marion Robert Morrison. Early in his career, the stage name "John Wayne" was chosen for him by movie director Raoul Walsh. Apparently, although "the Duke" never formally changed his birth name, he rarely, if ever, used it again, at least not in public.

I am also mindful of the nearly four million slaves in America, almost none of who had surnames before emancipation came in the wake of the Civil War. After the Thirteenth Amendment took effect in December 1865, freedom necessitated the choice of a surname. Many chose the names of presidents or famous statesmen, such as Washington. Jefferson, Jackson, or Franklin. Others reportedly chose the family names of their former masters. With some possible few exceptions, unlike me, none could ever possibly know the family names of their ancestors.

And how about all those German-Americans that changed their names during the First World War on account of anti-German sentiment, when, for instance, Braun became "Brown" and Schmidt was Anglicized to "Smith?"

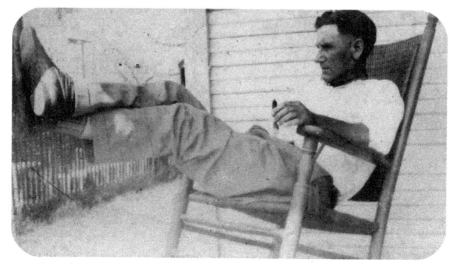

My "new" paternal grandfather, Charlie Miles, in a photo taken
when he was probably in late middle-age, about 1940 perhaps.

My paternal grandmother, Alice Tate Butler, in a photo taken about
1906 and one taken about 1940. I have no photos of her that were
taken in the 1920s.

Chapter Three
UNANSWERED QUESTIONS

Not unnaturally, this unanticipated discovery led me to form several questions to which I will almost certainly never have the answers, owing to the fact that absent any written confessions, of which there appears to be none, all the principals are long dead, and therefore can't be questioned.

Some things are easy to figure out. For instance, the reason why my grandmother decided to keep my father's paternity a secret, even if she wasn't entirely sure about it, seems quite clear. In a day and age when divorce was rare and for women, especially if they were guilty of infidelity, shameful, for my grandmother to openly admit her indiscretion would have almost certainly meant the end of her marriage, and of course if Charlie's wife, Lillian, ever found out, it would almost certainly have meant the end of his marriage also.

Furthermore, in that far-less-tolerant age, my father, even though an innocent child, would almost certainly been stigmatized by the circumstances of his birth and been called a "bastard," with both he and his mother becoming the subject of idle gossip and the object of scorn and derision by their neighbors.

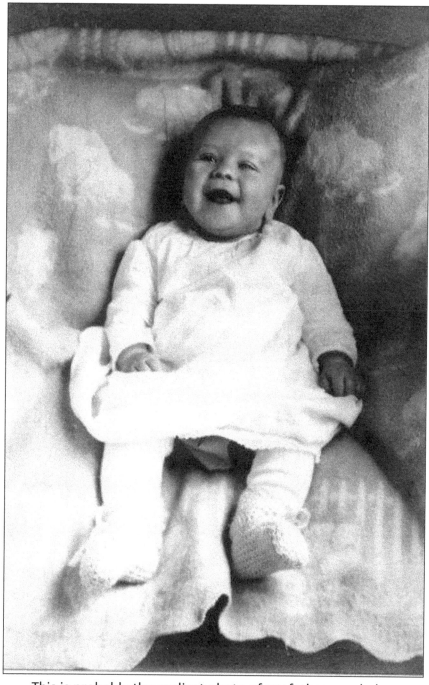

This is probably the earliest photo of my father as a baby.

Perhaps the most haunting question, however, is: *who knew what?*

Surely, even if my grandmother was uncertain about who was the actual father of her child, she must have at least realized that it *could* have been Charlie's.

By the same token. Charlie, who lived next door and therefore could not help but notice my grandmother's "baby bump" growing right before his eyes, must have wondered also if he was the father of his neighbor's child.

And what about Herman Butler? Did he know, or even suspect, that the baby to which his wife gave birth in 1927 was not his?

I also wonder: Did Charlie's wife, Lillian, know or suspect that something was going on, or had happened, involving her husband and next-door neighbor?

And what was the nature of the relationship between Charlie and Alice? Was it a one-time, encounter that was never repeated? Or, a long-term relationship that lasted for days, weeks, months, or even years? And did the couple love each other? Or, was it a matter of physical attraction only? Unfortunately, these are all unanswerable questions. All that we can be certain of is that Charlie and Alice engaged in intimacies at least once. The *when*, of course, is not hard to determine—clearly it had to be sometime in March 1927—nine months before my father was born in

December—but what were the circumstances that gave them the opportunity? One can only wonder.

The house at 1432 Rowan Avenue, where my father was born in December 1927. Could this also be where he was conceived? The Miles home, at 1426 Rowan Avenue, was to the left of this view.

I wonder too, did my grandmother and Charlie deliberately conspire to keep quiet about the child's paternity, assuming they knew or believed Charlie to be the father, or was it simply an unspoken agreement?

From all appearances, my grandmother's husband either did not know, or if he did, or even suspected, he chose not to allow my father's actual paternity to get in the way of treating the boy as his own child. Although my father's recollections of the man he thought was his dad were few, owing to the fact that Herman Butler died in 1935, when my dad was only seven, the memories of him that he shared with me from time-to-time were largely positive. One story that he often told was about the time that Herman took him fishing at White Rock Lake, and when my dad fell off the lower edge of the dam, where they were standing, Herman saved him from drowning. Another story my father liked to tell was about how Herman made him a homemade kite that was so large that when a gust of wind came along, my father, who was quite small at the time, was literally lifted up off the ground!

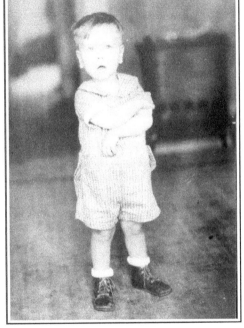

Right: A photo of my father, Raymond Joe Butler, at the age of about two.

My dad also fondly remembered how Herman, who was a carpenter by trade, made him a wooden desk that was similar to those that were used in schools.

The only story my father ever told about Herman in which there was even a hint of meanness was the time that an ice-cream truck came through the neighborhood and Herman gave my dad, who was probably a toddler at the time, a "slug," a small round blank piece of metal about the size of a coin, and then sent him out into the street to buy a treat with it. Of course, the ice-cream seller wouldn't take it, which confused my father, who did not realize that it wasn't real money. No doubt this amused Herman, who had a reputation as a joker. Not long before my father died, I asked him if Herman replaced the slug with a real coin, but he couldn't remember.

In any case, it comes down to this: Whether knowingly or unknowingly, it is an irrefutable fact that in effect, Herman Butler adopted my dad as his own son and gave him his surname.

Charlie, in contrast, is not known to have had anything to do with my father, even though he must have at least suspected the boy was his, lived next door to him until 1929, and even for decades afterward, never lived more than a mile or two away.

What makes this situation so sad to me was that when my father lost the man that he believed was his dad, his actual father was still alive, and would be until 1958, and therefore *could* have had a relationship with his son, but didn't. From conversations I had with my father over the years, it was clear, that as a boy growing up into a young man, he longed to have an adult male role model in his life, but never did.

Herman H. Butler, the man who in effect, whether knowingly or unknowingly, adopted my father as his own child. Photo taken about 1906.

Did Charlie not have anything to do with my dad because he wasn't sure that he was his father, and thought it better not to "rock the boat?" Or. did he stay away at my grandmother's request? Or. was it because he just didn't care? Again, these are questions to which I will almost certainly never have the answers.

I wonder too: Why didn't my grandmother tell her son the truth about his paternity at some point—when he reached adulthood, for instance, or least before she died? My father was only forty-four the year she passed away. I think he probably could have emotionally handled the news better *then*, than he would have at some later date.

Of course, the discovery of this secret also led me to have my own crisis of conscience. Should I tell my father? Or let him remain blissfully ignorant? My dad was ninety-one years old when I found out. Thinking that it would do him more harm than good, I decided to keep the secret, which I did until he passed away, never knowing the truth about his father. Everyone I *have* told, before and since his death, has agreed that I did the right thing.

****

Before I move on to the next chapter, I think a few words about how all this affected my view of my grandmother are in order.

First of all, Alice Tate Butler—who I called "Nannie"— was the only grandmother I ever knew, owing to the fact that my mother's mother died in 1934, fifteen years before I was born.

Secondly, from the time I was born until I reached adolescence, Nannie was my most frequent babysitter, in fact the only one that I can recall. Consequently, I have a wealth of memories of her. One that comes to mind is a spring or summer day when she was looking after me while my parents worked and I did something to displease her. I was either four or five years old at the time. To punish me for my misbehavior, she sent me to my room, shut the door, and then loudly announced from the other side that she was leaving, telling me that she couldn't stand to stay in that house a moment longer with a naughty boy like me. At first, I don't think I believed her, but then I heard the front screen door open and shut. In a panic, I jumped up from my bed, where I had been sitting, opened the bedroom door and ran to the front door, thinking I would see her walking away down the sidewalk, leaving me all on my own, but curiously, for some reason I couldn't see her. At first, I was puzzled. I didn't think my grandmother could walk *that* fast!

Then, and I'm not sure why, perhaps I heard a stirring, I turned around, and to my surprise, there was Nannie sitting on the living room sofa, smiling and watching me. *At once, I realized that she had only open and shut the door to make it sound as if she was leaving!* In the next moment I was in her arms, tearfully apologizing. Being the kindly, loving woman that she was, she comforted me, kissed me on the cheek or forehead, and told me that everything was all right, that she would never actually leave me alone. Naturally, it made me feel a whole lot better about things, and it may have led me to become a little better-behaved besides, although I can't say I'm one hundred percent sure about that!

Another time, she and I were walking together to the shopping center near the house in which my parents and I lived, when we witnessed an accident that occurred when the ball that some children were playing with rolled into the street, and one of the kids went chasing after it. At that very moment, a car driven by a woman, whose little boy, slightly younger than me, was standing up in the front seat (this was in the 1950s, long before seat belts were mandatory), suddenly braked, to avoid hitting the kid that had run into the street. Unfortunately, this had the effect of hurling the driver's little boy off the front seat and right into the windshield.

Taking me by the hand, Nannie looked to be sure there were no other cars coming, and then we rushed over to the stopped car, to see if something could be done to help. The woman was frantic because her little boy, who now had a big, bloody gash in his forehead, was screaming and crying. Very calmly, Nannie handed the woman a clean handkerchief (my grandmother always carried a clean handkerchief in her handbag) to wipe the blood away, after which the woman tried to return it to her. Nannie told her to keep it and advised her to take her son to a doctor right away, which the woman said she would, and then we continued on our way, as if nothing much had happened!

Nannie also acted as my nurse when I was sick. I still remember having chicken pox when I was four or five, and she jokingly told me that I must have contracted it from a stuffed toy chicken that I had in my room!

Nannie also took care of me when, at the age of eleven or twelve, I suffered through a week-long bout of Scarlet Fever. On this occasion, I stayed with her, at the house on Rowan Avenue, because the doctor said I was highly contagious and needed to be kept away from other people. As it happened, Nannie had had Scarlet Fever herself, when she was a little girl. Consequently, she was immune, unlike my father, my stepmother, and most of my friends and classmates.

It was awful. My skin turned bright red, and I ran a fever. My throat was so sore I could only eat mashed potatoes—made soft with milk—or alternatively, vanilla ice cream, which was usually half-melted, owing to the fact that my grandmother's refrigerator (she called it an "ice-box") didn't work very well.

Nannie told me than when she had Scarlet Fever, at one point she lost consciousness and her breathing became so shallow that her mother thought she had died. Thankfully, her mother—my great-grandmother, Sarah Tate—had the presence of mind to place a small mirror beneath my grandmother's nose, and when it fogged up, she knew that her daughter was still alive.

I told my grandmother that if anything like that happened with me, I hoped she would do the same thing!

After my parents divorced and my father remarried, I often spent entire weekends at my grandmother's house on

Rowan Avenue, where she kept a supply of toys and well-worn comic books to keep me amused, and where she fed me just about anything I wanted to eat. I was easy to please, however. Fried fish sticks, mashed potatoes and peas (Nannie always called them "English peas") was one of my favorite meals.

From time-to-time, my grandmother and I would walk together to the shops on East Grand Avenue, which were situated on either side of the street, between Samuell-Grand Park and the old Ford Motor Company plant on East Grand. On the way there, we might stop at the barber shop near the corner of East Grand and Barry, where she would wait patiently, the only woman in the place, while I got a haircut. Then, after stopping at the bank and Woolworth's, where she would stock up on inexpensive candy like circus peanuts and candy corn, we might go on to Brownie's, a café with "homestyle" cooking, where she would treat me to another of my favorite meals—sliced roast turkey on a slice of white bread, smothered in gravy, with mashed potatoes (also smothered in gravy), and "English peas" of course (still my favorite vegetable).

Occasionally, we would also travel together, by bus, to downtown Dallas, where the Walgreens drugstore in the Wilson Building, at Elm and Ervay streets, was one of Nannie's favorite places to shop.

Sometimes, when the mood struck her, Nannie would tell me stories about her childhood. One that I still remember is how one day, when she was perhaps nine or ten years old, she and some of her playmates, both boys and girls I think, were crossing a railroad trestle on foot, when a train approached at relatively high speed. To get out of the way of the fast-moving steam locomotive, all the kids jumped from the trestle into the nearly dried-out bed of the creek beneath it—except my grandmother! Afraid of heights (even though it really wasn't *that* far down), she thought fast and laid down on the tracks, huddled between the rails, and let the train pass over her, which must have been a terrifying experience!

Another time, Nannie told me, she and some kids were playing around on a fire engine at a nearby fire station when the alarm sounded. With no time to get off the horse-drawn vehicle, the frightened little girl stayed aboard, hanging on, she said, for dear life as it raced through the streets of Dallas!

At night, usually Saturday night, I would sleep next to her in her snug, quilt-covered cast-iron bed, and on Sunday morning, I could always look forward to a hot breakfast of something tasty like biscuits with grape jelly, and slices of meaty Canadian bacon.

After I became a teenager, and Nannie became older and frailer, more often than not, instead of me staying with her, Nannie would come to spend the weekend with us—me, my father and stepmother and my two half-brothers—at our home in a Dallas suburb. Because I had separate twin beds, she would sleep in my room, where the record player she bought me for a twelfth birthday present took pride of place.

Later, when I was serving in the Navy, Nannie was one of the few people I stayed in touch with regularly, by letter and postcard. One of my favorite photos of her was taken in the nursing home where she went to live in 1967, which shows a framed photo of me in my uniform on her nightstand and a souvenir Puerto Rico pillow cover, which I bought her, on one of the cushions on her rocking chair.

In short, I adored my grandmother, and I know she loved me, because she not only told me, but also demonstrated it in the kind, affectionate way that she always treated me.

This then, is the only image that I had of my grandmother—as a sweet, little old lady—until the day that I learned about the secret that she and Charlie Miles had taken to their graves!

I think for most people, the thought of their parents doing what's necessary to make babies is a little unsettling, much less their grandparents, *but let's face it, if none of them had done so, then none of us would be here now!*

I had already had a little bit of a surprise when, several years ago, I discovered that my grandmother's first child, a little boy that didn't survive infancy, was born only seven months after she and Herman were married. When I was young, I thought that in the past, people were more careful to conform to what was considered proper behavior. I know now that like a lot of things I was taught or led to believe in my youth, that just isn't true. Clearly, my grandmother and Herman did not practice abstinence before marriage, and I believe it is a near certainty that her pregnancy was the reason *why* they got married, which was not so uncommon in the past as one might think.

But to imagine my Nannie, at the age of forty-one, having an extramarital relationship with her next-door neighbor, well, I think that may be one of the reasons why the discovery of it hit me so hard at first. It just didn't fit with my image of her as a dutiful wife and mother, and a sweet, affectionate grandmother.

Nevertheless, that's clearly what happened, and in the end, I came to realize, it was a good thing too, or obviously I wouldn't be here now, writing about it!

But it also leads me to ponder another unanswerable question: *Why?* My Aunt Margaret once told me that toward the end of Herman's life, her parents had a less-than-blissful marriage. Perhaps he spent too much time away from home, taking part in KKK activities, leaving my grandmother to seek attention from another man, and Charlie, who lived right next door, just happened to be nearby, and receptive. It is equally possible, of course, that what happened was non-consensual, with shame and guilty feelings on both sides being the reason for silence.

Me and my "new" cousin, Beverly, at her wedding in September 2019; author photo.

Chapter Four
GETTING TO KNOW MY "NEW" FAMILY

As arranged by text message, I met my "new" cousin, Beverly Lumpkin, for the first time, at TGI Fridays in Mesquite, Texas, near Town East Mall, at 11:30 a.m. on Friday, April 19, 2019, for lunch.

Not unnaturally, I think we were both a little trepidatious. What I often say about never knowing what you're going to get with ancestors can be equally applied to living relatives, but in this case, I needn't have worried.

Thankfully, Beverly turned out to be a warm, welcoming woman whose charming smile and sense of humor, almost immediately put me at ease. It was clear to see that she was equally comfortable with me, and even before our lunch was ordered, we were talking to one another as if we had been acquainted all our lives.

Beverly, who is a little less than two years older than me, was very open about her life, telling me that she had been married twice, that she and her first husband had a daughter together, but due to incompatibility, they divorced. She went on to say that she and her second husband had been happy together, but sadly, he had died only a few years earlier. Presently, she added, she now had a new man in her life, who she intended to marry in the not-too-distant future (which she has since done).

One thing that delighted me was learning that Beverly and I were both educators, although with some differences. Beverly had taught in middle school, whereas I am a college professor. She is also retired, which I'm not (even though I am well past retirement age). The subject she taught was different too. Beverly's specialty was math, whereas I teach history.

Of course, I reciprocated by telling Beverly all about my life and my family too.

One thing that I was eager to know was whether or not anyone in Beverly's family had any idea that Charlie had fathered a fourth child by a woman to who he was not married. No, she told me, no one apparently had any idea, the same as in my family (so far as I know).

Over lunch, Beverly went on to acquaint me with my "new" family by telling me about her parents and also about her aunts and uncles—who were mine too, of course—and also about her cousins—also mine—of which she, or rather we, had only a very few since none of our grandfather Charlie's legitimate children had been especially prolific.

Beverly's mother—the oldest daughter of Charlie and his wife, Lillian Dalton—was Willie Mae Miles, a woman who did not get married to Beverly's father, Osborne Wright, until she was in her late thirties. Together, they had only one child: Beverly, who had been born in northern Louisiana, where her father was from.

Although our Aunt, Lorene Miles, married earlier in life, she and her husband likewise had only one child—a cousin, of course, to both Beverly and me—who so far as I know is still alive and well, but as of this date, is someone I have not yet had a chance to meet.

Our Uncle Roderick Vernon Miles, or just "R. V." for short, likewise had just one child with his wife, Marie—a son named Vernon Ray—who sadly died of cancer in middle age.

Although Beverly did not know a lot about our grandfather, Charlie Miles, owing to the fact that she was only ten years old when he died in 1958, she had at least spent some time with him, not one-on-one, but at family gatherings mostly, which of course I never had the chance to do, nor my father. However, she had some photographs of him and other family members, which she brought to our meeting in a large scrapbook she had assembled and decorated herself. Naturally, I was eager to have a look at it, although Beverly had already sent me a few photos attached to text messages.

Something that I have always found curious was how little my father resembled his supposed father, Herman Butler, so naturally, when I first got a chance to take a closer look at a photo of my "new" grandfather, I was curious to see if he looked anything like my dad. I was especially interested to see if my father's overly-long earlobes—a physical trait that was evident even in childhood photos—were a genetic gift from his actual father, and it appears that they *were*, although Charlie's seem not to have been quite as long as my dad's.

Beverly also had some photographs of Charlie's mother—our great-grandmother, whose maiden name was Margaret Elizabeth Hodge. One, a formal portrait. showed her sitting with her second husband—Charlie's stepfather, Seaborn E. Jones—and their children—Charlie's seven half-brothers and half-sisters. Two others showed her on her own. In none of these photos was she smiling. I got the impression she either had bad teeth and didn't want to show them, or was just a very unhappy person.

The photograph that excited me the most was actually a photocopy of a newspaper clipping taken from the now-defunct *Dallas Journal*, dated January 22, 1925. In an earlier text or email to Beverly, or perhaps to my cousin Henry Butler, I had wondered whether or not the Miles children and the Butler children were playmates. Since they were close to the same age and lived next-door to one another, it seemed to be highly likely. Well, when I saw the newspaper clipping, I could hardly believe it! Here was the proof!

In the photo, which is entitled "The Kids in Our Block," there are eleven children of various ages, and also a horse. On the front left, standing right in front of Beverly's mother—Willie Mae Miles—is Ruth Butler, my father's then-nine-year-old sister! Of course, Willie Mae was my dad's sister too, or rather half-sister, as was Ruth. Our uncle, R.V., my dad's older half-brother, is also in the photo, holding the bridle of the horse. The text below the photo lists their names, addresses, and parents' names.

When I later shared a digital scan of the photo with my cousin Henry, he replied in astonishment: "You can't make this stuff up!"

****

On Easter Sunday, April 21, 2019—two days after my lunch with Beverly—I decided to drive out to Laurel Land Memorial Park, in the Oak Cliff section of Dallas, to visit Grandpa Charlie's grave.

Interestingly, Charlie had never lived in Oak Cliff, but Uncle "R.V." had, which is why Charlie and his wife, Lillian, were both buried in the same cemetery as "R. V." and his wife, Marie.

Although Laurel Land is a huge, sprawling cemetery, I didn't have too much trouble finding Charlie's grave, having done some research on the Find-a-Grave website beforehand, and while I hadn't gone there specifically to find anyone else's grave, I couldn't help but notice that my "new" Aunt Lorene and her husband, Ed Bailey, were buried only a few steps from Charlie and Lillian.

On the way home from Laurel Land, I decided to take a slight detour and visit Forest Lawn Cemetery in Northwest Dallas, where my grandmother, Alice Tate Butler, was buried, along with her husband, Herman, her parents, and her unmarried sister, Mamie, who doted on my father when he was young.

Visiting Charlie's grave on Easter Sunday, 2019; author photo.

I was dismayed to see that the lot where the five of them are buried was under at least an inch of water in some places, including all five headstones, on account of some recent thunderstorms, and also the fact that over the years, the ground had dipped below its original height. I wasn't surprised, however, because I knew from previous visits that it had been like that whenever there were heavy rains, for at least the past twenty years.

Suddenly it struck me; instead of just putting up with the situation year-after-year, as the family had done, perhaps it was time to do something about it!

Soon after, when I next visited my father in the retirement home to which he had recently moved, I mentioned the situation at the cemetery and suggested that we ought to see about doing something about it. My father, who had seen the submerged lot himself several times in the past, agreed, so I wrote a letter to the cemetery manager to find out what could be done and how much it would cost, if anything.

In mid-May, the cemetery manager contacted me by email, to let me know that bringing the ground level up would cost nothing because they could simply use any excess soil that was left over the next time a burial occurred, but that as a consequence, the headstones would have to be reset, to bring them up to the new level. The cost: $150 per headstone, for a total of $750. When I passed this information on to my dad, he agreed to bear the cost and wrote a check, which I immediately sent to the cemetery manager.

Whilst all this was transpiring, I became aware, from my own observation and also from the original 1925 deed, which had come into my possession, that the lot contained six spaces, but that only five had been used, which the cemetery manager confirmed by email when I asked him about it.

Not long afterward, I took my dad to see the lot, which was not quite as submerged as it had been on Easter Sunday, but was still a bit "swampy," and while we were there, I suggested to him that he claim the last remaining space in the lot that his maternal grandfather had purchased in 1925—two years before he was born. I had already asked the cemetery manager about it. and he had informed me there would be no problem, provided that the space had not been inherited by anyone else. I assured him it hadn't, and that as the oldest surviving grandchild of the original purchaser, my father not only was the person most entitled to it, but also the family member most likely to need it in the foreseeable future. After Dad agreed that it would be better to be buried near his parents, grandparents, and an affectionate aunt, rather than by himself in a remote spot in the vast expanse of Restland Memorial Park in northeast Dallas—as he had long ago planned for when the time came—on his behalf, I drew up an affidavit in which he claimed the unused space at Forest Lawn. After he had signed it in the presence of a notary public, I sent it to the cemetery manager.

It has since struck me that if I had not taken that DNA test, which led me to discover the truth about my dad's biological father, which then led me to visit Charlie's gravesite on that Easter Sunday, and also on the same day my grandmother's, we might never have thought about the fact that there was an the unused cemetery space at Forest Lawn, and my father, who has since passed away, would be buried instead at Restland.

****

After meeting Beverly, I wanted my father to meet her too, after all, they were uncle and niece, but how to do it without revealing the family secret? And what would be the best opportunity? I also didn't want to wait too long because he was starting to become frail and I couldn't be sure how much longer he would live or be able to get out, although I hoped he might reach ninety-six, the age of his oldest Butler sister, Margaret, when she passed away.

Fortunately, I didn't have to wait very long. On a sunny Saturday afternoon in June, shortly after my birthday, I hosted a picnic for family and friends at White Rock Lake Park in Dallas, which gave me the chance I wanted to bring my father and Beverly into contact with one another without revealing the family secret.

The guest list was small: In addition to me and my wife, there was an old high school buddy and his wife, the ex-wife of another old high school buddy, one of my half-brothers and his wife, my father, of course, and Beverly and her fiancé.

When Beverly and her husband-to-be arrived at the picnic site, a shady spot near the Bathhouse Cultural Center, by previous agreement with my "new" cousin, I introduced her as fellow professor whose grandparents, by coincidence, had once lived on Rowan Avenue in East Dallas, next-door to my father's family. The first part was a little white lie, of course, but the second part was not untrue, although unsurprisingly, my father did not remember the Miles family at all, since he was only two years old when they moved away. But that was expected. For me, the best part of the day was seeing my father and his niece together in the same place, although, of course, he did not, and never would, know her true identity.

Here is a portion of a group photo, showing, from left to right: My "new" cousin, Beverly, my oldest half-brother, Daryl, my father, Raymond Joe Butler, and me, taken at White Rock Lake Park, Dallas, Texas, June 2019; author photo.

When Beverly showed the newspaper clipping to Dad, the one in which his sister Ruth is standing in front of Beverly's mother, he found it interesting, but when he heard the name of his real father, Charlie Miles, spoken aloud, of course it meant nothing to him.

Unfortunately, although Beverly and I met up several more times during the summer and fall, either singly or with our partners, my birthday picnic was the only occasion when my father and his "new" niece were in the same place at the same time, except, sadly, his funeral, which came much too soon, only six months later.

CHAPTER FIVE
IN SEARCH OF CHARLIE

When I first started looking for my "roots" in the 1970s, genealogical research required multiple trips to the genealogical department of the downtown public library to examine books as well as microfilmed federal census and other public records, writing a lot of letters, and, all too often, road trips to distant county courthouses to pore over heavy, oversized books in which deeds, wills, marriages, etc. were recorded. Today, thanks to the Internet and websites like Ancestry, Family Search, Fold3, Find-a-Grave, GenealogyBank, and so on, a savvy researcher can uncover in a matter of hours the same amount of data that once took months or sometimes even years, to gather.

I once spent the larger part of a summer, in the early 1990s, transcribing the 1860 federal census for Freestone County, Texas. Today, it's available on any number of websites, some free, some by subscription. If I had known the Internet was only few short years away, I would never have wasted my time on it. But of course. I didn't know then what was coming in the not-too-distant future.

Not long after I learned the truth about my paternal lineage, and gathered some information from my "new" cousin Beverly, I began doing one of the things that I do best—family history research—and, thanks to the fact that so many records are online now, I was able to make rapid progress.

The person I most wanted to know about, obviously, was my "new" grandfather, Charlie Miles. What was he like? Where did he come from? What did he do for a living? Some of the answers to those questions turned out to be quite surprising.

One thing I quickly learned was that Charlie and my grandmother, Alice, were almost exactly the same age, both born in 1885—Charlie on August 18 and Alice on September 9. When their extramarital relationship, or whatever else it can be called, occurred, they were both forty-one years old, and forty-two when my father was born. And neither was a native Texan. Charlie was born in Tennessee and Alice in Alabama.

They were also married to their respective partners very close to the same time—my grandmother, Alice, in 1906 and Charlie in 1908.

Likewise, Charlie and Alice had the same number of children with their marriage partners: three—as well as the same ratio of male to female, namely two girls and one boy, although not in the same birth order. Alice's oldest child was her son, Henry, born in 1908. Charlie's oldest was his daughter, Willie Mae, born in 1909. Alice's daughter Margaret was next, in July 1910, and almost exactly a year later, in July 1911, Charlie's daughter,

Lorene, was born. Lorene was followed by her brother, Roderick or "R.V." in 1913. Alice's youngest daughter, Ruth, was born in 1915. My father, therefore, was technically an only child, because he was the one and only offspring of both Charlie Miles and Alice Tate Butler—and he had six siblings, or actually half-siblings, not just the three that he knew about.

Charlie and Alice also moved to Rowan Avenue, in East Dallas, at nearly the same time: The Miles family arrived about 1919, the Butler family in 1920.

****

In my search for Charlie, I also encountered some amazing coincidences. Since 1977, I had believed that my paternal ancestral home in Texas was Fairfield, the seat of Freestone County, where my supposed great-great-grandfather, Alfred Butler, and his family, had settled in 1854, after first residing in nearby Palestine for two years. As a consequence of this belief, I had not only visited Fairfield several times, but also researched, wrote, and self-published a brief history of the town, which I and my father and my oldest son visited together in the summer of 2002, to commemorate the one-hundred and fiftieth anniversary of the Butler family coming to live in Texas, spending the day visiting the Freestone County museum, the cemetery where Alfred Butler is probably buried, and the location of his 100-acre farm. All this activity was in addition to spending a summer transcribing the 1860 federal census for Freestone County, as mentioned elsewhere in this book.

So, what does this have to do with Charlie? Well, after I began to research the life of my "new" grandfather, I discovered that he had obviously come to Texas sometime between 1900—when he was enumerated in the federal census for Franklin County, Tennessee—and 1908, when he and his wife, Lillian Dalton, were married by the Reverend George Truett of the First Baptist Church in Dallas, and then went to live, according to a notice in the *Dallas Morning News*, in the town of Richardson—*the very same Dallas suburb in which my family and I have made our home for the past thirty-six years!*

In short, owing to my being completely unaware of Charlie and Alice's secret until 2019, I had completely misidentified my paternal ancestral home in Texas for more than forty years, *while unknowingly living in the correct one for nearly that same amount of time!*

Not surprisingly, Richardson was a much smaller place in 1908 than it is today, measuring then no more than five or six blocks square. Unfortunately, I have so far been unable to ascertain the Miles family's precise address, but I would be willing to bet that I drive past Charlie's house, or the site where it once stood, or certainly at least within a few blocks of it, nearly every day, and have done for years— and also the site of the livery stable in which he once worked, just two blocks north of Main Street.

Here are some more remarkable coincidences:

Between 1976 and 1977, my wife and oldest son and I lived in an apartment complex located off Royal Lane in a section of northwest Dallas, called "Field City," just a mile or so south of Farmers Branch—another Dallas suburb. During my research into the life of my "new" grandfather, I discovered that he had worked for most of his adult life as a construction supervisor for the Dallas County Road and Bridges Department. And where, of all places, was the county shop located, the one that Charlie drove to every workday for decades? On Joe Field Road, about a half-block from where my family and I were living back in the late 1970s!

Here's another coincidence. First, think of all the possible occupations a person could have. There must be thousands, right? From 1913, or possibly earlier, until he retired in the early 1950s, Charlie was a road building supervisor. Well, as it happens, I am not in the same line of business as Charlie, but my oldest half-brother, Daryl, is!

Finally, there is the fact that in 1958, when Charlie's funeral was held, not in Dallas, where he lived for most of his life, but at the Rhoton Funeral Home in suburban Carrollton, my father was living in that city, where he and his second wife had only recently bought a home!

****

In mid-May 2019, about a month after my "new" cousin, Beverly, and I first met, I made my first Miles family-related road trip. Accompanied by my youngest son, I drove to Fort Cobb, Oklahoma, a remote little town out on the Great Plains, some two hundred and thirty miles or so north of Dallas. There, we visited the little country cemetery where Grandpa Charlie's mother—my great-grandmother—was buried in 1942, beside her second husband, Seaborn Jones, who died much earlier, in 1909.

While standing there in the middle of this little cemetery, located on a vast, nearly treeless prairie, miles and miles from any larger city, I could not help but wonder: What possessed them to leave the lush, green hills of middle Tennessee to live in this particular spot, of all the other places in America to which they could have gone? Perhaps someday, I'll find the answer. *Or not.*

****

Shortly after returning home from Oklahoma, where my youngest son and I also visited one of our favorite spots, the beautiful Wichita Mountains National Wildlife Refuge, we hit the road again. This time my son and I were bound for Franklin County, Tennessee—Grandpa Charlie's birthplace!

I'd been to Tennessee before, on at least three other occasions, but it had been more than a dozen years since my most recent visit.

A little less than two days after leaving home, my son and I arrived at Winchester, the seat of Franklin County, where, after checking into the motel we had booked in advance, we went for a hike in the Short Springs Natural Area, near Tullahoma, in neighboring Coffee County. There, after a mildly arduous trek through a beautiful, green forest—so strikingly different from the Oklahoma plains—we beheld a beautiful waterfall, with the odd name of Machine Falls, located in a little valley shaded by tall trees of just about every imaginable kind.

The next morning, my son dropped me off at the Franklin County Courthouse, where I spent the morning looking for deed and probate records relating to the Miles Family and some of the associated families that I had already discovered through online research. Afterward, I visited the local library's genealogy room, where I was assisted in my search by a knowledgeable local historian.

Unfortunately, as I discovered to my dismay, many of the earliest county records, dating back to the 1800s, were no longer kept in the country courthouse, but in a special archive building that was only open one day a week, and it was unfortunately *not that day*, nor even the next. I did, however, obtain the name and phone number of the archivist, from the historian at the library, who assured me that if I phoned the archivist after returning home, she would be more than willing to help me, which I afterward learned was very true.

Here I am outside the Franklin County Courthouse in Winchester, Tennessee, May 2019; author photo.

My son and I spent the remainder of our time in Tennessee exploring and hiking in some of the beautiful state parks and natural areas of the state, where we saw more waterfalls in a few days than I think I had ever seen in all my life up to that point.

And all the while, I could not help but wonder, why on earth would someone leave all this natural beauty and move to the flat lands of North Texas or Oklahoma? At the same time, I also thought that it was a good thing that Charlie *had* made the move, or I would not even exist!

****

Following our return from Tennessee, I spent most of my spare time over the next two months doing online research, and I am happy to report that thanks to the Internet, I was able, in a relatively short amount of time, to build a new family tree that not only replaced the old one, but also exceeded it in the number of branches.

Speaking of branches: There is probably nothing more boring than hearing someone tell you all about their ancestors, especially if they weren't particularly colorful or famous or important, but before I move on to the next chapter, I feel compelled to do just a little bit of bragging. Thanks to my most recent research on the Miles and associated families, I now know that I am not only descended from one of the earliest settlers of colonial Virginia, a man named Christopher Branch, but also that I am distantly related through Branch's granddaughter, to Thomas Jefferson, third president of the United States and author of the Declaration of Independence.

How cool is that?

CHAPTER SIX
EPILOGUE

By coincidence, on the very same day that I uncovered my grandmother and Charlie's secret, my father vacated the rundown Lake Highlands apartment that had been his home for thirty-three years, and moved into a much more comfortable residence at the Bentley Retirement Home on Forest Lane in North Dallas, only a few blocks from the house in which he had lived with his second wife from 1967 to 1979.

During the almost eight months that my father enjoyed his new apartment, my brother Daryl and sister-in-law, Ginger, who live not far from the Bentley, visited Dad on a nearly daily basis, to keep him well-supplied with snacks, to do his laundry, and help him out with whatever else might need doing. Then, on Monday, November 11, 2019, Daryl found Dad unconscious and with no pulse or evident breathing. After the paramedics that he summoned revived our father and got him breathing again, he was taken to nearby Dallas Medical Center, where he lingered, unconscious, but still breathing, until he passed away on Wednesday, November 13, at about 8:40 in the morning. Both my half-brothers were with him when he died. I arrived about 45 minutes after they phoned me, while I was teaching a class at Collin College in Plano.

Dad's funeral was held in Dallas, Texas, at the Restland Funeral Home Memorial Chapel, located in the funeral home's administration building. It was held there because he had prepaid his funeral arrangements (in 1986), expecting for many years to also be buried at Restland, in the new Freedom Garden section on the south side of Restland Road. However, earlier this year, as noted in a previous chapter, Dad had decided instead to be buried at Forest Lawn Cemetery in Dallas, where his mother, a devoted aunt, his maternal grandparents, and Herman Butler, the man that Dad had believed to be his father, are all buried, since there was one unused space in the lot that Dad's maternal grandfather, I. H. Tate, had purchased more than ninety years ago.

Prior to the service, Dad's casket, which sat atop a bier at the front of the chapel, was open so that people could come up to see him. There were also photos of our father on tables near the entrance. I brought three: One of him and my oldest grandson, playing with a toy car on the floor of Dad's Lake Highlands apartment, one that was taken when Dad was in the Navy, and another in which he was wearing the exact same Boy Scout leader's uniform that he was wearing in his casket. Dad had told me and my two half-brothers many times over the years that he wanted to be buried in his Scout uniform, and so he was.

Before the service, my wife and I went up to the casket, which was open, at the front of the chapel. We were standing there by ourselves as I stroked Dad's hair and said goodbye to him for the last time, when I'm not ashamed to say that I started sobbing. Some of my sorrow, I think, came from being aware that I knew something very fundamental about my father's life that he never knew himself, and never would.

After the service began, the casket was closed, and a large American flag draped over it. The casket was supposedly copper in color, but it looked more like a light chocolate brown to me. The handles were silver in color.

With the funeral director—a tall, slender woman—leading the way, the family entered the chapel at 2:30 p.m., with my wife and me right behind her, followed by my two half-brothers and their wives, a nephew, and my former stepmother—Dad's second wife. We all sat on the very first row.

As we entered the chapel and took our seats, a song, "Time Waits for No One," as recorded by the Hilltoppers in 1954, was playing over the chapel's speakers. I chose it for the service because several years ago, after Dad attempted to play it on an out-of-tune piano that we encountered on one of our outings, he told me it was his "theme song." It was the only music played or performed at the service.

A Presbyterian minister from the church where Dad was a member officiated. I am not religious myself, nor is my wife, but Dad was, as are my half-brothers and almost certainly most of the other people who attended, and I knew that Dad would have wanted a religious service, so that's what we had.

I do not know the names of everyone who attended. Many were people from Dad's church that I do not know, but before the service started, I did see and speak to several friends and family members, including my "new" cousin Beverly and the man she had only recently married.

After the minister read some scripture, etc., he called me up to the pulpit and I read the eulogy I had written for the occasion, nearly word-for-word as I had composed it, and, remarkably, without breaking down into tears.

The minister then read some more scripture, quoting from the Book of Ecclesiastes, about there being a season for everything, etc. He also read a poem I had given him earlier, which I found among Dad's personal belongings. It said, in essence, that a man with a lot of friends was a success in life. It had accompanied a photo of Dad and one his post-divorce girlfriends, who had given it to him, writing on it that in her eyes he was a success.

Then, as prearranged, the officiating minister invited all the former Boy Scouts in the chapel to come forward and recite the Scout Oath as a tribute to Dad's fifty years of service as a Boy Scout, Cub Scout, and Explorer leader. There were seven, including me and my two half-brothers. At least two—my brother, Daryl, and an old high school buddy of mine—were former Eagle Scouts.

From thereon, the service was entirely in the hands of the minister, who conducted the standard sort of Protestant Christian service that one might expect, full of references to Jesus, and promises about resurrection, life everlasting, and so on. At one point he mentioned the book of Revelation in the Bible, and quoted some more scripture, most of which I didn't listen to very carefully since I was mostly staring at my dad's casket and thinking about him, and how I would never ever see him again.

The service lasted about forty-five minutes, which was less than the hour or so I had expected. After we followed Dad's flag-draped casket out of the chapel, it was loaded into a black hearse, parked just outside the chapel door. Then, after my half-brothers and I, and our wives, had chatted a while with some of the other mourners, we got into two waiting limousines for the drive to Forest Lawn Cemetery, located at the corner of Walnut Hill Lane and Harry Hines Boulevard in northwest Dallas.

At Forest Lawn, we parked near the lot where Dad was to be buried. There were still a lot of tree limbs and debris in the cemetery, the result of a tornado which had cut a sixteen-mile-long-swath across much of North Dallas and part of Richardson a little more than three weeks earlier, but thankfully, the immediate vicinity of the gravesite was clear. There was a small blue canvas marquee with seats beside the site, which I hadn't expected. I sat in the front row of seats, in the middle, flanked by my sister-in-law, Ginger. on my left, and my wife on my right.

The graveside service started at about ten minutes to four p.m. It was a beautiful fall day. The sun was out and very bright, with hardly a cloud in the sky, and the air temperature was probably in the mid-70s, Fahrenheit. The service consisted of the minister briefly speaking about the hope of everlasting life, etc. again, followed by a military ceremony performed by two Navy Chief Petty Officers that consisted of one of them playing "Taps" on a bugle while we all stood and either put our hands over our hearts, or saluted if we were veterans. I saluted of course, and very nearly broke down into tears again as the bugler played. I did weep a little, but managed not to sob, with my wife putting her arm around me to comfort me and hand me a tissue.

After the final notes of "Taps" drifted away into the stillness of the air, we sat down while the two Navy chiefs removed the flag from Dad's casket, folded it carefully, and then saluted it in turns while the other held it. Then the tallest one asked who was to receive the flag. As pre-arranged with my brothers, I indicated with outstretched arms that it was me. The Chief then knelt in front of me, looked me directly in the eye, and presented the flag to me in the name of the President of the United States and a grateful nation for my father's service. Then, he and the other chief departed.

After the pallbearers and me were invited by the funeral director to put our white boutonnieres on top of the casket and to throw a handful of dirt into the grave, we watched as Dad's casket was lowered into his grave beside the grave of the man who for his entire long life he had believed to be his actual father.

****

Saturday, December 21, 2019, would have been my father's 92nd birthday. To commemorate it, I had lunch by myself at the El Fenix Mexican Restaurant in Casa Linda Shopping Center—the same restaurant where I had treated him to lunch on his birthday every year (or almost every year)—since he turned sixty-five. And every year, I would tip off the waiter that it was my Dad's birthday. Then, without fail, except for one time when they were short-staffed, four or five members of the wait staff would come to the table after we had finished our meal, present Dad with a hot sopapilla covered with cream and strawberry sauce, and sing "Happy Birthday Dear Panchito" to him. Later that day, just before sunset, I visited Forest Lawn Cemetery—where he was now buried—to sprinkle some earth from the front yard of his birthplace on his grave. I had scooped up a little for that purpose back in February, when he and I had visited the now-vacant site of the old homestead in East Dallas. (The idea originated from the time in 1995 when Dad and I stopped at the site of my mother's birthplace in Muskogee, Oklahoma, and I took a little soil for her grave on our way to her funeral in Chicago.) I didn't think then, however, that I would need it so soon. Even though he was ninety-one at the time, I had hoped Dad would live for at least another three or four years, but it turned out to be only a few months instead.

In the evening, my two half-brothers and I, and their wives, and a nephew and his wife, gathered at Daryl and Ginger's house to remember our father and to celebrate his life. After enjoying some barbecue from the restaurant where we had taken our dad to lunch on Father's Day every year for the past two decades, we sat down to watch a thirty-seven-minute long tribute to Dad, which I made myself, using bits and pieces of video that I had recorded over the past few years. Parts of it were funny, but by the time it ended, almost everyone in the room had tears in their eyes, including me, who, I'm not ashamed to say, had already wept once before, when I previewed it at home.

Finally, after eating some birthday cake that I wished my father could have been there to enjoy with us, I revealed the secret I had only learned about some nine months earlier, and which I had thought I might have to keep to myself for years: That a DNA test I took had shown that our paternal grandfather was *not* the man that our dad had thought was his dad, and that *our* dad was instead the result of an extramarital relationship of some kind, involving our grandmother and her next-door-neighbor on Rowan Avenue in East Dallas, a man named Charlie Miles.

I also told them that I had decided it was best not to tell our father, believing that emotionally, it might have done him more harm than good to have such information so late in his life. My brothers agreed I had done the right thing.

Before telling them all this on our father's birthday—a day that I decided was the most appropriate for that purpose—I had worried about how they would react to this news. To my relief, they were not only unfazed, but also curious to know more about our "new" grandfather, Charlie Miles, so I obliged them by telling them everything I had recently learned, and then showed them digital images of the photographs that our "new" cousin, Beverly, had shared with me. In short, I needn't have worried.

****

So, am I sorry that I found out? The answer is "no." I would rather know the truth than to keep on wasting my time and effort, seeking ancestors who aren't really mine. I just wish I had known a lot sooner!

That being said, *where do I go from here?* As noted elsewhere in this book, I have already done a lot of online family history research, and have also made two family history research trips that were rewarding experiences. Thanks to the wealth of documentary records that are now available online, I am hopeful that in time, I will be able to add even more "new" branches to my family tree, to grow the ones that are already there, all the while keeping my fingers crossed that no further family secrets come to light that result in the need for additional pruning!

CHAPTER SEVEN
BUT WAIT, THERE'S MORE!

In mid-January 2020, just as I thought I had finished saying everything I wanted to say in this book, I made another startling discovery about the Miles family that I think is worth sharing with my readers.

In Chapter Two, I mentioned that when I received the results of my Ancestry DNA test in 2015, I noticed four individuals with the surname Miles in my list of matches, *and*, as I also pointed out, I decided not to contact them at that time because they each had posted a family tree online that made it clear (or so I thought) that even though we were obviously related, it appeared that our earliest common ancestor was someone who had lived in the distant past, probably the eighteenth century. Yet one of these matches, as I further remarked, was identified as probably a second cousin, which would place our common ancestor a little closer in time, perhaps the nineteenth century. Nevertheless, I just couldn't see the connection.

Before I go any further, I need to add that thanks to the online research I did in 2019, after uncovering Charlie and Alice's 91-year-old secret, I learned that Charlie Miles' father was named John W. Miles, and that he had married Charlie's mother, Margaret Hodge, in Franklin County,

Tennessee on October 20, 1884. Charlie was born the following year, on August 18.

I also learned that in 1893, Charlie's mother had married a man named Seaborn Jones, by whom she had six more children—Charlie's half-siblings—and that sometime after 1900, Margaret and Seaborn left Tennessee and ended up in Fort Cobb, Oklahoma, where Seaborn died in 1909, and where my youngest son and I visited his and Margaret's grave sites in May 2019.

But what had become of Charlie's father, John W. Miles? With nothing else to go on, I just assumed he had died sometime between 1884, when Charlie was conceived, and 1893, when Charlie's mother remarried.

Now, I must return for a moment to the four people named Miles in my list of DNA matches. The family trees that each of them had posted online were more or less identical, showing that their line of descent was from a man named John Henry Miles, and from him to his father, John W. Miles, whose own father, they all agreed, was a man named Samuel A. Miles.

Of course, I couldn't help but notice the name John W. Miles in their family trees, but from all appearances, he was an entirely different John W. Miles to the one in my family tree. Why? Because my John W. Miles was born about 1845, and his father's name, I also discovered through my research, was William B. Miles, whereas *their*

John W. Miles was born in 1837, and was the son of Samuel A. Miles. To distinguish between the two men, I called theirs "John #1" because he was apparently the older of the two, and I called mine "John #2."

The two Johns also had different mothers. The mother of John #1, according to the family trees posted online, was a woman named Rebecca, whereas the mother of John #2 was a woman named Mary Farrar, which I had verified through Franklin County, Tennessee probate and court records.

In an effort to keep things organized, I made a two-column chart. On one side, I wrote the names of the people in my list of DNA matches that traced their ancestry through John #1, and on the other, I wrote the names of a slightly smaller list of matches through John #2.

At this point, I reasoned that someday I would find the distant ancestor that was common to both lines and I would then be satisfied that I knew how I came to be related to the descendants of John #1 as well as John #2.

Unfortunately, that's the extent of all I managed to accomplish in this regard, *until I made the unexpected discovery that not only solved a mystery, but also brought my family history into clearer focus!*

Before I reveal the breakthrough that I made in January 2020, I need to mention further that before Charlie was born, his father, John W. Miles, had already been married twice. By his first wife he had a son, William A. Miles, who was Charlie's older half-brother. Apparently, John's first wife died, because when William was still a child, John married a woman named Kate, who he sued for divorce in 1884, on the grounds of her alleged adultery. He and Kate had no children together. Later that same year, after John's divorce was granted, he married Charlie's mother, Margaret. who as I have previously pointed out, remarried in 1893, and then started a whole new family with Seaborn Jones.

But as it happens, Margaret was *not* a widow in 1893, as I had earlier assumed.

On January 17, 2020, while doing some further online research about the Miles family, by chance I learned that in 1892, in Franklin County, Tennessee, Charlie's mother, Margaret, had sued John W. Miles for a divorce, which was granted, thus clearing the way for her to legally marry Seaborn Jones.

So why could I not find any further evidence of John W. Mile's residence in Tennessee? Simple: *He wasn't there!*

As I read the various county court documents relating to Margaret and John W's divorce, I could hardly believe my eyes! According to both Margaret and other people who were called as witnesses, John W. Miles had abandoned his wife and son in December 1885, when Charlie (who was mentioned by name and age in one of the documents) was only four months old!

Although neither Margaret nor any of the witnesses could say for certain where John W. had gone, they all agreed that he had disappeared some seven years earlier, and all believed that he had gone first to Alabama, and then on to Texas, either sending for or taking with him a certain "lewd woman" named Alice Hefner, with who, they said, he had apparently been consorting both before and after his marriage to Margaret, and with who he had fathered some other children.

As I read this sad story of betrayal and abandonment, the name Hefner rang a bell. I had seen it before. *But where?*

And then it struck me: I had seen it in the family trees of those four individuals named Miles to who I am a DNA match! And when I checked to be sure, there it was: *Mary Alice Hefner*, the wife of the very same John W. Miles from who they were all descended, a man who had nine children with Mary Alice, with whom he had lived in Collin County and Hunt County, Texas from 1898, or slightly earlier, until his death in 1928.

After I saw John W. Miles' death certificate, which stated that he was born in Tennessee and that his father's name was unknown, but that his mother's maiden name was Farrar, I knew I finally had it figured out. *John #1 and John #2 were in fact the very same man!*

But what about the father of John #1 being Samuel A. Miles? And what about John #1 being born in 1837? There is a simple explanation: Those were obviously honest mistakes, as often happens when people do family history research, and also when relatives provide information for the death certificates of people older than themselves, which is clearly what happened when John W. Miles died in Greenville, Hunt County, Texas in 1928. The person who provided information for John W. Miles' death certificate, a son-in-law named Kay Walker, said that John W. was born in 1837, which is the birth year that was afterward erroneously engraved on his tombstone in the I.O.O.F. (International Order of Odd Fellows) cemetery at Caddo Mills, Hunt County, Texas. Precisely why Walker thought so is unknown, but it was mistaken nonetheless.

Further research has revealed that much of what the divorce court witnesses said was correct. John W. Miles had indeed fathered three children with Alice Hefner before abandoning Charlie and his mother (one of them was born a month after Charlie). They were also correct about him going to Alabama (where two more children were born), but the rumor that Margaret told the court, about John and his son, William A. Miles, killing a man in Alabama, which resulted in the son in jail while John became a fugitive, was clearly just that, a rumor. At least no evidence of such a thing has turned up. *But who knows?*

The witnesses were also obviously correct about him going to live in Texas, which he did sometime between the birth of his and Alice's fifth child, born in Alabama on April 7, 1892 and their sixth child, born in Texas on September 10 or October 10, 1893 (sources differ).

One source (the death certificate of John W. and Mary Alice's sixth child, Claud Washington Miles), also provides evidence that they may have initially lived in Johnson County (south of and adjacent to Tarrant County, where the city of Fort Worth is located) before moving in 1898 (or earlier) to Collin County, where they purchased 100 acres of land near the little town of Josephine, a short distance west of the cemetery where John W. Miles now lies buried. In 1901, John W. and his wife, after selling that acreage, bought a larger farm in adjacent Hunt County; but a year before Mary Alice died in 1916, they were living again in Collin County, at Josephine, where in 1920, the federal census taker found John W, a farmer his entire life, residing with his youngest daughter, Pearline, a.k.a. "Perry."

Sometime after the 1920 census was taken, but before John W. died in 1928, he apparently went to live in Greenville, Texas with another daughter, Novella, who was then married to a man named Rufus Kay Walker—the person who was directly responsible for the erroneous birth year (1837) written on John W.'s death certificate as well as engraved on his tombstone.

What's interesting to me about all this newly-discovered information is that not only did it solve the mystery of how

I am related to all those previously inexplicable DNA matches, it also raises some questions about Charlie and his father, John W.

First and foremost is: Did Charlie, who lived in Dallas County, Texas from sometime between 1900 and 1908 until his death in 1958 know that his father was living, until 1928, only forty miles north, in neighboring Collin and Hunt counties? Likewise, did John W. know that the son he abandoned as an infant was living in the next county?

And if either one knew, did Charlie or his father ever attempt to have anything to do with the other? In short, *were they ever reconciled?* Or did they each just go about their daily lives, completely unaware of how close they were in terms of miles? (No pun intended.)

Another question it raises is how could John W. abandon little Charlie in his cradle, and then go on to responsibly raise another nine children with his fourth and final wife (if indeed they were ever legally married)? How could he be such an irresponsible, seemingly uncaring parent to one and not to all the others? This, of course, is also the same question we can ask about Charlie, who never had anything to do (so far as we know), with the child—my dad—that he fathered with Alice Tate Butler. If by some chance he knew for certain that my dad was his child, did he look to his own father's example to rationalize his non-involvement?

Unfortunately, just like the questions that I posed in Chapter Three, for obvious reasons these too will have to remain unanswered.

****

Solving the mystery of how all those other Miles cousins fit into my family tree was certainly gratifying, but the realization that my "new" great-grandfather had lived and died and was buried in a place that was only a 45-minute drive from my home was even more exciting to me, especially considering that I had previously assumed that he was probably lying in an unmarked grave in who-knows-where, Tennessee.

Those who know me best will not be surprised to learn that at my earliest opportunity, only two days after this most recent discovery was made, I went to take a look. Thankfully, the weather cooperated.

So, on the afternoon of Sunday, January 19, 2020, a mild sunny day, I drove to the home of my cousin Beverly Lumpkin, who I had invited to come along with me (after all, John W. Miles was her great-grandfather too), and then we headed out on Interstate 30 toward Caddo Mills, Texas, the Hunt County community which is nearest to the I.O.O.F. Cemetery where our great-grandfather, John W. Miles, is buried.

Because I had "done my homework," so to speak, we had no trouble finding the cemetery, but unfortunately, although it was smaller than a lot of cemeteries I've seen, it wasn't tiny either.

While Beverly waited in the car, looking through the folder of papers about John W. that I had brought along, I went searching, on foot. for his grave site. Thankfully, someone had already posted a photo of his marker on Find-a-Grave, so as I tramped about the cemetery, at least I had some idea of what I was looking for, and fortunately, it was an upright marker, the type that are obviously easier to find than ground-level markers.

I searched first on the northwest side of the cemetery, where some of the oldest markers seemed to be. Then, I went over to the northeast side, and to my great satisfaction, found what I was looking for in a matter of minutes.

After returning to the car to tell Beverly, "I found him!", we walked together to the site where our great-grandfather was buried beside his fourth wife, Mary Alice Hefner. One of their oldest sons, Layton M. Miles, is buried in the same row, just one space further along.

As we stood there, looking for the first time at our great-grandfather's grave marker, I pointed out to Beverly that the dates of birth and death engraved on it were wrong, because according to federal census records and other sources, John W. was almost certainly born about 1845, rather than 1837 as the marker said. Unfortunately, as I mentioned previously, an ill-informed son-in-law, Rufus Kay Walker (husband of John W.'s daughter, Novella Miles), of Greenville, Texas, had served as "informant" for his father-in-law's death certificate.

Remarkably, I added, not only was the birth year almost certainly erroneous, but also the birth and death dates on the marker did not match the death certificate information! On the death certificate, John W.'s date of birth is given as December 14, 1837, but the marker inscription reads "December 4, 1837." Likewise, the death certificate states that he died on May 17, 1928, whereas the marker says "May 27, 1928."

I noticed that the birth year on the marker for John W.'s son, Layton, was likewise wrong. It reads 1881, but numerous reliable sources say 1884.

As it happens, this sort of thing is not uncommon. For example, when my grandmother Alice's husband, Herman H. Butler, died in 1935, she acted as informant for his death certificate, giving 1878 as his year of birth, which was afterward engraved on his marker. In fact, he was born in 1880. But there it is to this very day, "1878" literally engraved in stone! Unfortunately, this sort of mistake is a lot more difficult, and obviously more expensive, to correct than writing on paper.

Cousin Beverly Lumpkin and me, at the grave site of our great-grandfather, John W. Miles, in Hunt County, Texas; *author photo.*

After taking some photographs of the stones by themselves and of us standing beside them, we got back into the car and headed for the little town of Josephine, only three-and-a-half miles to the west.

In 1904, when our great-grandfather and his fourth wife and their children lived on a farm near Josephine, which straddles the Hunt County-Collin County line, the town's population was 400. Today, 1,296 people live there, which is obviously three times the population a century ago, but still quite small.

There isn't much to see in Josephine either, but to prove that we had actually been there, Beverly and I stopped at a little park next to City Hall, where we used my tripod and the timer on my camera to take a photo of ourselves standing beside a Texas Historical Commission marker that gives the history of the community, which was founded in the late 1880s. I remarked to Beverly that although our great-grandfather and his family were not among the very first settlers in the area, a land deed dated 1898 provides proof that they weren't very far behind.

Before leaving Josephine, we drove to Thelma Street, where John W. had purchased a city lot in 1915, the year before his wife, Mary Alice, died. There is no house on the lot today, but we speculated that there must have been one there in 1915. Either that, or John had one built.

From there, we head northwest out of Josephine, to see the site of our great-grandfather's first farm in the area, a 100-acre spread located about three-and-a-half miles from town. Remarkably, it is still farmland today, typical of North Central Texas—in other words, very flat and featureless, except for a row of trees that were almost certainly planted as a windbreak.

Unfortunately, we missed seeing the sign for the county road that would have taken us back to Josephine in a matter of minutes. As a result, we ended up driving twice as far as we needed to go, passing through the equally small town of Nevada before eventually returning to Josephine. But this time, we didn't stop. Instead, we kept going for another mile, crossing the line into Hunt County, and then turned right on to a smooth, but unpaved road. After pulling over to the side for a moment, to take a look at the 160 acres of farmland our great-grandfather bought in 1901, we went on down the road a further mile or so to Josephine Cemetery, where John Henry Brown, one of John W.'s sons by his fourth wife, is buried. Fortunately, the cemetery was very small and John Henry's marker was easy to find.

And then we headed back to Dallas County, retracing the route, more or less, that we had taken earlier that day.

****

So, as I said at the conclusion of the previous chapter, when I thought I was done with this book, *where do I go from here?*

The answer is the same: Whenever time permits, I'll keep on researching my family's history, with a view to tracing as many lines back as far as I can, compiling the information and the stories that I hope to leave as a legacy for my children, my grandchildren, my newfound cousins, and for all our as-yet-unborn descendants, so that they don't have to wonder, as I once did: "Where did we come from? Only this time, thanks to a simple DNA test that led to a surprising result, combined with the most recent discovery described in this chapter, it appears I'm even more firmly on the right road!

OTHER POOR SCHOLAR TITLES BY STEVEN R. BUTLER

John Neely Bryan: The Father of Dallas

From Water Supply to Urban Oasis:
A History of White Rock Lake Park, Dallas, Texas

The Forgotten Soldiers

From London to Kentucky:
The Life and Times of James Haycraft, Jr. and his son,
Samuel Haycraft, Sr.

Guided by Reason: The Golden Age of Freethought in Texas

Available for sale on Amazon.com

CPSIA information can be obtained
at www.ICGtesting.com
Printed in the USA
FSHW010502071220
76659FS